Judicial Control of Administrative Action in India through the Writ of Certiorari

Dr. Amit Singh

LAXMI BOOK PUBLICATION
2019

Price: 800/-

Judicial Control of Administrative Action in India through the Writ of Certiorari

Dr. Amit Singh

© 2019 by Laxmi Book Publication, Solapur.

All rights reserved. No part of this publication may be reproduced or transmitted, in any form or by any means, without prior permission of the author. Any person who does any unauthorized act in relation to this publication may be liable to criminal prosecution and civil claims for damages. [The responsibility for the facts stated, conclusions reached, etc., is entirely that of the author. The publisher is not responsible for them, whatsoever.]

ISBN- 978-0-359-58098-9

Published by,
Lulu Publication
3101 Hillsborough St,
Raleigh, NC 27607,
United States.

Printed by,
Laxmi Book Publication,
258/34, Raviwar Peth,
Solapur, Maharashtra, India.
Contact No. : 9595359435
Website: http://www.lbp.world
Email ID: apiguide2014@gmail.com

PREFACE

Society from the twentieth century onward has become complex and Government functions have multiplied. In fact the twentieth and the present century is the age of the Administrators. Dean Rescoe pound had observed that : "as the eighteenth and the forepart of the nineteenth century relied upon the legislature and the last half of the nineteenth century relied upon the courts the twentieth century is no less clearly relying upon the administration."

This state of affairs may be attributed inter-alia to the decline of the laissez-faire philosophy of Government which had its heyday in the nineteenth and early twentieth century with its notion that the proper role of governmental administration is the maintenance of a State which seeks to guarantee the individual a maximum of freedom from coercive influence and a protection against the more obvious types of anti-social conduct. In its place is a new awareness of the responsibility of the State towards the economic and social welfare of the nation, and in order to discharge this responsibility. it became necessary to bring these myriad activities under the regulatory power of the Government. The preamble to our constitution with its infaces on social justice and the Directive Principle of the State in India. The attempts of our Governments, Central and State of achieve this ideal have resulted in immense increasing legislative output and the expansion of administrative action into fields previously uncovered.

This in its term has given rise to the problem of Controlling State Action to ensure that the rights of individual are safe guarded against arbitrariness on the part of the administration. The law relating to the subject including pleading, procedure and practice is its exhaustively dealt with and judicial decisions scrutinized and analyzed. During the last hundred years the conception of proper sphere of governmental activity has been completely transformed.

The Modern State has assumed the role of social Welfare State. Today, the activities of State are not mere regulatory. Vigorous industrialization, concentration of large sections of population in over-crowded cities created problems of housing, disease, smoke, insecurity of life. that could not be ignored. The administration had to intervene in the interest of public safety. This brought a change in the role of administration. To meet these requirements administration has to be armed with legislative and judicial functions. The technical nature of dispute gave rise to adjudicator/power to administrative agencies. This all clearly shows a tremendous growth in powers of administration.

The extension of the executive arm of government into all spheres of activity necessarily results in greater interference with the rights of private individuals and although it is incontrovertible that ample powers must be conferred on the executive for it to function effectively, yet it cannot be denied that it is imperative that there should exist some form of check to prevent the exercise of these powers from degenerating into pure arbitrariness. Thus arming the administration with such vital functions required some reasonable check and control over their exercise, because in absence of a check, there is a constant danger of its assuming the role of dictator or what C.K. Allen describes as "Bureaucracy triumphant", Griffin has also written : "most important problem of our time : the relationship between public power and personal rights. We are concerned, then, not merely with powers and processes of the Administration, but with the control of the Administration, legal and political, without which that essential balance between individual liberty and public good is impossible"

This necessitated innovation of certain remedies to steer clear of the impediments to the realization of personal rights. Among all other sources writs also formed and still form a powerful means for constituting the remedial function of the law. To evaluate the circumstances leading to the innovation of various types of writs the query has to haul back to the twelfth and thirteenth centuries when the prerogative writs were issued, by the Royal courts in exercise of their prorogation. By virtue of these writs the King's Bench Division of the High Court of England assumed jurisdiction which Blackstone called 'very high and transcendent: "It keeps all inferior jurisdictions within bounds of their authority, and may either remove their proceedings to be determined before itself or prohibit their progress below. It commands magistrates and other to do what their duty requires in every case where there is no other specifice remedy. It protects the liberty of the subject by speedy and summary interposition.

      Sir C.K. Allen says that now a days the most common use of certiorari is to require the inferior tribunals to 'hear and determine' a cause which they have refused to entertain, and to compel the local and public utility authorities to carry out their duties. In India before the existence of the present Indian Constitution administrative decision were mostly discretionary. This discretionary attitude of administrative authorities is now being regulated with the help of certain provisions of the Constitution of India. The Indian Constitution makers envisaged a welfare State with wide extensive of the administrative process. The Constitution-makers also incorporated in the Constitution certain provisions which invested the courts with broad powers of review. The Supreme Court exercises control over administrative authorities under the Article 32 and 136. Article 32 empowers Supreme Court to issue Constitutional writs. directions and orders for the enforcement of Fundamental Rights of citizens. Article 226 empowers the High Courts to issue Constitutional writs etc. to protect Fundamental Rights and also "for any other purpose". Here the words "any other purpose" means the enforcement of anylegal rights. The writs can be issued by the High Courts within their territorial jurisdiction, to any person orauthority including in appropriate cases any Government. A High Court can also issue a writ against any Government inappropriate cases, though it is not situated within its territorial jurisdiction, but cause of action arose within its territorial jurisdiction. Thus the constitution sought to provide the safeguards against the extended powers of administration and various High Courts control the Administrative process through their writ jurisdictions. The judicial review of administrative action has therefore constitutional sanction behind it in India.

Of the various remedies in the nature of writs against governmental action which developed during the course of time the writ of certiorari is one. The remedies so far investigated deal with the control of powers. The prerogative writ of certiorari is the most generally useful weapon to control judicially administrative action. English judges traced the origin of this writ which was originally in the hands of the sovereign to the direction in Magna carta that the crown was bound neither to deny justice to any body nor to delay any body in obtaining justice. The work attempts to a study in same detail the Judicial Control of Administrative Action in India through the writ of certiorari, the method examined is the one extra ordinary legal remedy. The examination of the method has been made historically and analitically.

Owing to the intricate and complex system of Government that exists in a modern state and the vast extension of social legislation that has taken place in modern time with last flew decades and unprecedented growth of the administrative process has taken place. The problem arising out of this development have become the most important issue of law at present because they have affected many aspects of the legal system. In the name of efficiency and quickness the rights of individuals could be arbitrarily taken away by conferring powers on the executive. The grant of large powers to the Governments is incompetable with the rule of law. (Howers) The Committee on Minister's Powers declared that: "no consideration of administrative convenience are executive efficiency should be allowed to weaken that control of the courts and no obstacle should be placed of Parliament in the way of the subjects unimpeded access to them." (Report P. 114) It was pointed out at uncontrolled power was apt to be abused. Judicial control of administrative action is needed essential by all informed opinion. Administrative action requires supervision from three points of view; the points are view of public welfare, administrative efficiency and private interests immediately affective by the administrative action. To-day in India the need for Judicial Control is perhaps at the maximum. It has a illegacy of countries of foreign hegimony. At the same time, there is no organized and affective option against the Government. The only agency, therefore, to keep up the balance is the judiciary which is to point out to the executive what is its rightful domain and like the angle with the framing swords present it from overstepping." (Chagla CJ., Law, Liberty and Life, (1950) pp.24-25) Briefly stated, this work is a study of the judicial control of administrative action in India exercised through the writ of certiorari. The purpose of this study is to make an attempt to analyze the practice of judicial control of administrative action through the writ of certiorari. As far as possible, original sources of information have been consulted. Certiorari is an order issued by a superior courts asking authority or inferior courts to transmit the records of proceedings some cause are action to the superior court for its consideration. This writ mainly goes to judicial or quasi-judicial body. But in many cases, a serious violation of people's right may be made by an administrative agency, which may not come within definition of judicial act Courts can quash order of the administrative authority either on error of law apparent on the face or an excess or abuse of jurisdiction, Certiorari is however not available if the decision of agency, is not based on an substantial evidence. Certiorari is discretionary or may be granted when the impugned act is on face of it erroneous or raises question of jurisdiction or infringement of the fundamental right of the petitioner." A writ of certiorari can be issued against even a mere administrative body if its executive order is not inconformity with the rule of Jaw and if it is outside its powers. Rules of natural justice have to be observed and the authority should have applied its mind. If the impugned order negatives this factors. certiorari can issue."

If there is some other specific and sufficient remedy then the question of certiorari normally does not arise. In addition. is well established that the negligence on the part of persons on hose behalf an applications has been made will exclude the issue of the remedy. These limitations have been adversely commented by le scholar of English speaking words. All this led Prof. Davis to say lither parliament or the law Lords should throw the entire set of prerogative writs into the Thamos river, heavily weighted with sinkers to prevent them from rising again." Lord Denning also in s Hamlyin lectures said "just as the pick and shovel is no longer suitable for the winning of coal, so also the procedure of mandamus, certiorari and action on the case are not suitable for the winning of freedom in the new age."

But inspite of these defects it is felt that certiorari is still a beneficial remedy. It requires certain reforms and such reforms are suggested as under: It is submitted that the audi atteraum portem should apply to every case where the person or property of a private individual is adversely affected by the decision of an administrative agency and that regardless of whether the decision be characterized as "judicial", "quasi-judicial", "administrative" or one affecting only a privilege and regardless of the extent to which discretion may be involved. The test should be that of the effect upon the individual concerned. It seems that in England and India, the binary courts of law have reached the limit of their inclination to enforce a general standard of procedural fairness in the exercise statutory powers. Fifty years ago it could have been said that Doctrine of Audi Alteram Pattern had great potentialities for growth. It does not seem that such hopes can be entertained today in the U.S.A the law has been carried some way beyond the point where English Law stopped short in the Arlidge case, and in several countries of the commonwealth the general principle that statutory powers may be exercised only after fair hearings is now well established. See, for example, the Canadian case - L'Alliance des Professor Ethioliquers V. Labour Relations Board of Quchec. It submitted that so far as India and England are concerned, it would be useful to enact a simple and general code of procedure, a kind of administrative bill of rights in the light of needs of twentieth and twenty first centuries The first provision of this should be that no man's liberty, livelihood or property could be taken from him unless he had first been heard in his own defence, and that this should apply to all statutory powers in default of express provision to the countrary. Exceptions would have to be specified, for their powers such as the power to arrest a suspected criminal, which are in a different class from those to which natural justice applies. And legislative powers, which affect the public generally and not merely one or more individuals, would have to be excepted. The United states of America has not only the due process clause of the constitution, which applies in such cases, but also the Federal Administrative Procedure Act of 1946. An example of the combined effect of the Fourteenth Amendment and the Administrative procedure Act in enforcing the essentials of fair procedure is Vong Yang Sung V. McGralii (1950). In France it is also the case at the power, for example, to cancel a license cannot be legally exercised without giving a proper hearing to the person affected.

Some Observations regarding India

In India we find lot of corruption and maladministration within administration, particularly maladministration is wide spread, and it can be said that the lack of appeal system within the administration is the cause for that. While officials have been armed with a lot of unlimited powers and discretion, corresponding rights of individual have not been evolved in proper manner Here we do not have such inquiry like Frank Committee in England to look in to e deficiencies of administrative justice. The present inadequacy of the administrative structure and the individual helplessness against authority in the matter of securing administrative justice have been widely recognized. The fact remains that the existing remedies against abuse of authority by administration particularly in lower echelons are not available to 5 common man, for whom concept of equality before the law and social justice have at present little significance or value All these things necessitate greater judicial control and this can be done by judicial creativeness by the courts.

The judgements of the courts exhibit lack of creativeness. As we have seen that Indian courts have practically followed the principles of English law governing the writ of certiorari inspite of wide language used in Art 226. It is urged that political, social and economic conditions in India differ widely from England. Again integrity in administration, expertise knowledge of tribunals, strong public opinion, council on tribunals and Ombudsman etc., strengthen the administrative justice in land while in India we lack these things it is urged that Judges must take into account all these things living law of a community requires that it should take into account social facts and legal norms of a community should be able to meet particular needs of the community. It is high time that sound principles in the spheres of administrative justice should be evolved in the light of Indian conditions. Our Administrative Law should be Indianised rather then following English Law. It is regretted that the courts in India e practically transplanted English Law governing the writ of certiorari without applying their mind, whether certain rules of English law are suitable in India under the present context. It is submitted that a thorough investigation should be made regarding utility and relevance of English rules governing the writs in India. As it is interesting to note that English rules relating to certiorari have n criticized by English men themselves. It is urged that Supreme Court should take a pragmatic approach as Mr Justice Holmes once said that "Life of Jaw is not logic but experience".

All this necessitate a code of Administrative procedure in India e fight of present state of affairs, that is, such rights are to be created in the individual as not to Jeopardised social welfare programme and economic planning of the State. Till such code is created, it is submitted, that there is a need greater judicial control over administrative process. The dignity of man and significance of his freedom are the essential postulates democratic way of life which the Constitution heralded and this never be achieved without justice. social, economic and political enshrined in our Constitution. In solving the problems that front the path to socio-economic justice, liberty and freedom judges have to clay their role without fear or favour, uninfluenced by consideration of dogmas or isms. Judges are the upholders of the dignity, defenders of liberties and protectors of rights under the common law as well as the rights guaranteed by the Constitution. There must be judges in the land, says Lord Denning "who are no respectors of persons and stand between the subject and any encroachment on his liberty by executive".

Judges by their decisions, have contributed greatly to the moving and developing laws; and present day society Iged to democratic way of life looks eagerly and sincerely for their decisions on Jaws to have the liberties of the people safe-guarded against all invasions either by the State or by any authority individual. Legislative, Executive and Judiciary are the three limbs of government, of these three, judiciary is the most important because it has a supreme task of striking a balance among executive, legislative and the people. Thus the judges have prominent part of playing in order to keep the democratic way of life a progressing. The law as instrument of social change does not become fully effective unless certain conditions are satisfied. The primary condition is the creation and maintenance of good law enforcement machinery, which would command the confidence of the people and be fair. quick and operable at cost, which the age citizen can afford.

The preamble of our constitution secures to all citizens social, economic and political justice and also equality of status and opportunity. The rule of law also requires that poor and illiterate persons should be assisted enforcing their rights. Article 39-A also des that State shall ensure justice on the basis of equal opportunity to all citizens. Because of these reasons the locus standi concept has been relaxed and any public-spirited person has been allowed to file public interest litigation in good faith for preventing the violation of the rights of the poor. It is, therefore, submitted that in "to prevent violation of rights of disadvantaged persons the public interest litigation ruled be encouraged. In some foreign tries also the concept of PIL is being encouraged. Here, it will not be out of place to mention that recently Mr Aharon Barak. Chief justice of the Israeli Supreme Court said at New Delhi before a gathering which included many judges of the Apex Court of India what would the Supreme Court of India do if a PIL was Bled seepaing direction to the Prime Minister to sack a minister who has been indicated of corruption? He further said that in all probability, it will dismiss the PIL questioning the locus standi whereas the Israeli Supreme Court, in a similar matter, has directed the Prime Minister of country to sack an indicated minister. He further said that in matters of public importance every Israeli has been standi warrant whereas in India even in case issue of writ of quo-warranto, Allahabad High Court has recently held that although the principle of locus standi is to an extent relaxed in a writ of quo-warranto but it is not abondoned altogether. These must be some connection between the petitioner and the appointment be challenges. It is thus submitted that PIL should be encouraged and in matters of public importance every Indian should have locus Standi. However, inspite of the limitations and short comings stated above the prerogative remedies in India have been largely availed by the people to their great advantage. Article 226 of the Constitution has made the people feel that the State exists primarily for their good and that under its laws they have rights of which they can obtain quick enforcement by the highest court in the state at a very reasonable cost. Not only this in case of violation of Fundamental Rights they can obtain quick justice by the Apex Court of Country at a very reasonable time and cast and the courts do justice to the individual citizen while giving due weight to the requirements of the public interest and they fearlessly enforce the principle, that government must be carried on strictly in accordance with the law. It is, however, submitted that the scope of certiorari should be widened by adopting. The principle that administrative fact findings unsupported by substantial evidence should be liable to be quashed and any error of law involved in an administration decision should be capable of correction by certiorari even through it is not apparent on the very face of the record should be capable of correction by certiorari even through it is not apparent on the very face of the record.

Dr. Amit Singh
Head of Department (Law)
M.J.P. Rohilkhand University, Bareilly

ABBREVIATIONS

A.C.	:	Appeal Case
A.I.R.	:	All India Reports
A.L.J.	:	Allahabad Law Journal
All E.R.	:	All England Law Reports
Andhara L.T.	:	Andhara Law Times
Bomb. H.C.Rep.	:	Bombay High Court Report
C.L.R.	:	Common Wealth Law Reports
C.W.N.	:	Calcutta Weekly Nots
Camp. L.J.	:	Company Law Journal
Ch. D.	:	Chaucery Division
Comb L.J.	:	Cambridge Law Journal
D.L.R.	:	Dominion Law Reports
E.R.	:	English Reports
I.C.	:	Indian Cases
I.Eq. R.	:	Irish Equaty Reports
I.L.R.	:	Indian Law Reports
I.R.	:	Irigh Reports
JILI	:	Journal of the Indian Law Institute
K.B.	:	Law Reports King's Bench
L.D.R.	:	Law Quarterly Review
L.R.	:	Law Review
Lab. L.J.	:	Labour Law Journal
Lal & I.C.	:	Labour and Industrial Cases Mad
L.R.	:	Modern Law Review
P.C.	:	Privy Council

Q.B.	:	Queen's Bench
S.C.	:	Supreme Court
S.C.R.	:	Supreme Court Reports
T.L.R.	:	Times Law Reports
W.L.R.	:	Weekly Reports

CONTENTS

SR. NO.	CHAPTER NAME	PAGE NO.
	INTRODUCTION	01
1	HISTORY, ORIGIN AND MEANING OF 'PREROGATIVE WRITS'	7
2	ORIGIN, HISTORY AND NATURE OF CERTIORARI	28
3	SCOPE OF CERTIORARI	42
4	GROUNDS ON WHICH CERTIORARI WILL LIW	61
5	PROBLEM OF LOCUS-STANDI IN CERTIORI	118
6	CONCLUSIONS	127
	SELECT BIBLIOGRAPHY	134

INTRODUCTION

Society from the twentieth century onward has become complex and Governmental functions have multiplied. In fact the twentieth and the present century is the age of the Administrators. Dean Roscoe Pound has observed that:

'........ as the eighteenth and the forepart of the nineteenth century relied upon the legislature and the last half of the nineteenth century relied upon the courts, the twentieth century is no less clearly relying upon the administration.[1]

This state of affairs may be attributed inter-alia to thedecline of the laissez-faire philosophy of Government which had its heyday in the nineteenth and early twentieth century with its notion that the proper role of governmental administration is the maintenance of a State which seeks to guarantee the individual a maximum of freedom from coercive influence and a protection against the more obvious types of anti-social conduct. In its place is a new awareness of the responsibility of the State towards the economic and social welfare of the nation, and in order to discharge this responsibility, it became necessary to bring these myriad activities under the regulatory power of the Government.

The preamble to our constitution with its infaces on social justice and the Directive Principles of the State policy in envisage the establishment of a welfare State in India. The attempts of our Governments, Central and State to achieve this ideal have resulted in immense increasing legislative output and the expension of administrative action into fields previously uncovered.

This in its term has given rise to the problem of Controlling State Action to ensure that the rights of individual are

---

1. Pound "The Administrative Application of Legal Standards" (1919) 44. A.B.A. Report 445, 446.

safe guarded against arbitrariness on the part of the administration.

The law relating to the subject including pleading, procedure and practice is its exhaustively dealt with and judicial decisions scrutinized and analysed.

During the last hundred years the conception of proper sphere of governmental activity has been completely transformed. The Modern State has assumed the role of social Welfare State. Today, the activities of State are not mere regulatory. Vigorous industrialisation. concentration of large sections of population in over-crowded cities created problems of housing, disease, smoke, insecurity of life, that could not be ignored. The administration had to intervene in the interest of public safety. This brought a change in the role of administration. To meet these requirements administration has to be armed with legislative and judicial functions. The technical nature of dispute gave rise to adjudicatory power to administrative agencies. This all clearly shows a tremendous growth in powers of administration.

The extension of the executive arm of government into all spheres of activity necessarily results in greater interference with the rights of private individuals and although it is incontrovertible that ample powers must be conferred on the executive for it to function effectively, yet it cannot be denied that it is imperative that there should exist some form of check to prevent the exercise of these powers from degenerating into pure arbitrariness. Thus arming the administration with such vital functions required some reasonable check and control over their exercise, because in absence of a check, there is a constant danger of its assuming the role of dictator or what C.K. Allen describes as *"Bureaucracy triumphant"*, Griffth has also written :

".......... most important problem of our time : the relationship between public power and personal rights. We are concerned, then, not merely with powers and processes of the Administration, but with the control of the Administration, legal and political, without which that essential balance between individual liberty and public good is impossible.[2]

This necessitated innovation of certain remedies to steer clear of the impediments to the realization of personal rights. Among all other sources writs also formed and still form a powerful means for constituting the remedial function of the law. To evaluate the circumstances leading to the innovation of various types of writs the query has to haul back to the twelveth and thirteenth centuries when the prerogative writs were issued by the Royal courts in exercise of their prorogation. By virtue of these writs the King's Bench Division of the High Court of England assumed jurisdiction which Blackstone called 'very high and transcedent':

"It keeps all inferior jurisdictions within bounds of their authority. and may either remove their proceedings to be determined before itself or prohibit their progress below. It commands magistrates and other to do what their duty requires in every case where there is no other specifice remedy. It protects the liberty of the subject by speedy and summary interposition.[3]

Sir C.K. Allen says that now a days the most common use of certiorari is to require the inferior tribunals to 'hear and determine' a cause which they have refused to entertain, and to compel the local and public utility authorities to carry out their duties.[4]

In India before the existence of the present Indian Constitution administrative decision were mostly discretionary. This discretionary attitude of empowers the High Courts to issue Constitutional writs etc. to protect Fundamental Rights and also "for any other purpose". Here the words "any other purpose" means the enforcement of anylegal rights. The writs can be issued by the High Courts within their territorial jurisdiction, to any person orauthority including in appropriate cases any

---

2. Principles of Administrative Law, p.2. 3 Bl. Comm., 40-2.
3. 3 Bl. Comm. 40-2.
4. Law and Orders (1965) pp.216-17 Law in the Making(1964) p. 571.

Government. A High Court can also issue a writ against any Government inappropriate cases, though it is not situated within its territorial jurisdiction, but cause of action arose within its territorial jurisdiction. Thus the constitution sought to provide the safeguards against the extended powers of administration and various High Courts control the Administrative process through their writ jurisdictions. The judicial review of administrative action has therefore constitutional sanction behind it in India.

Of the various remedies in the nature of writs against governmental action which developed during the course of time the writ of certiorari is one. The remedies so far investigated deal with the control of powers. The prerogative writ of certiorari is the most generally useful weapon to control judicially administrative action. English judges traced the origin of this writ which was originally in the hands of the sovereign to the direction in Magna carta that the crown was bound neither to deny justice to any body nor to delay any body in obtaining justice.[5]

The work attempts to a study in same detail the Judicial Control of Administrative Action in India through the writ of certiorari, the method examined is the one extra ordinary legal remedy. The examination of the method has been made historically and analitically.

Owing to the intricate and complex system of Government that exists in a modern state and the vast extension of social legislation that has taken place in modern time with last flew decades and unprecedented growth of the administrative process has taken place. The problem arising out of this development have become the most important issue of law at present because they have affected many aspects of the legal system. In the name of efficiency and quickness the rights of individuals could be arbitrarily taken away by conferring powers

---

5. Per Bowen, L.J. in In re Nathen (1884) 12 Q.B.D. 463 cited with approval by Bhagawati, J. in Tan Bug Tain V. Collector of Bombay (1945) 8 F.L.J. 247 at 294.

on the executive. The grant of large powers to the Governments is incompetable with the rule of law. (Howers) The Committee on Minister's Powers declared that :

"no consideration of administrative convenience are executive efficiency should be allowed to weaken that control of the courts and no obstacle should be placed of Parliament in the way of the subjects unimpeded access to them." (Report P. 114) It was pointed out at uncontrolled power was apt to be abused. Judicial control of administrative action is needed essential by all informed opinion. Administrative action requires supervision from three points of view, the points are view of public welfare, administrative efficiency and private interests immediately affective by the administrative action. To-day in India the need for Judicial Control is perhaps at the maximum. It has a illegacy of countries of foreign hegimony. At the same irne, there -is no organized and affective option against the Government. The only agency, therefore, to keep up the balance is the judiciary which is to point out to the executive what is its rightful domain and like the angle with the framing swords present it from overstepping." (Chagla CJ., Law, Liberty and Life, (1950) pp.24-25)

Briefly stated, this work is a study of the judicial control of administrative action in India exercised through the writ of certiorari. The purpose of this study is to make an attempt to analyse the practice of judicial control of administrative action through the writ of certiorari. As far as possible, original sources of information have been consulted. The first chapter of this THESIS deals with the history, origin and meaning of prerogative writs. In this chapter history of writs in England and in India as well as writ jurisdiction of courts in India have been discussed.

The second chapter deals with the origin, history and nature of certiorari. The history of certiorari in England, history and development of certiorari in India and nature of certiorari have been dealt with in this chapter.

The third chapter discusses the scope of certiorari including distinction between judicial, quasi judicial and administrative decisions and also the meaning of the term duty to act judicially.

In the fourth chapter the grounds on which certiorari is issued have been discussed in detail.

The fifth chapter deals with problems of locus-standi and in the last chapter conclusions and suggestions have been given. Thus it is an humble attempt to focus the attention of those who are concerned with application an appreciation of the writ of certiorari in the system of judicial review. Briefly stated, this work is a study of the writ of certiorari as method of judical review of administrative acts in India.

1 Chapter

HISTORY, ORIGIN AND MEANING OF TREROGATIVE WRITS

(A) ORIGIN AND MEANING OF 'PREROGATIVE WRITS'

The prerogative writs are the means by which the courts exercise judicial control over administrative actions. Where an administrative action is ultra virus it can be controlled by these writs. Also failure to carry out a duty imposed by statute on an administrative agency affords grounds for interference by the courts. Royal courts exercised supervisory jurisdiction over inferior courts through prerogative remedies which were originally granted by the King, as the "fountain of justice", and by virtue of the royal prerogative. They were therefore known as the 'prerogative writs'. Thus, the origin of writs is embedded in the history of common law and judicial institutions in England.

The word writ is equivalent of the Latin 'brave'. In substance both the words refer to the same thing though to different aspects - the English to the fact that it is in writing. the Latin to the fact that it is short and terse. These expressions were used, in the course of time, in the form of a letter directed to some named individual. The word 'brief', derived from 'brave', was used in the sense of a letter in Germany. Certain authors are prone to attribute the origin of writ to the Saxon time 'gerwrit'. Subsequently 'writ' came to be know as a Royal order drawn in concise terms and put in writing. Blackstone defines a writ as "a mandatory letter from the King in Parliament, sealed with his Great Seat, and directed to the Sheriff of the country wherein the iNucy is committed or supposed to be requiring him to command the wrong doer or party accused, either to do justice to the complaint, or else to appear in court, and answer the accusation against him".[1]

Charter defines the writ as -

"It was the King's order to his liege, written on parchment and sealed with the Royal Seal, and disobedience of the writ was contempt of the Royal authority, and punishable as such"[2]. Because of being an extraordinary judicial discretion of the King in council, these writs were originally intended for the use of the crown only. Thus a written order issued in the name of the King was a writ. In the course of time these writs were also available to subjects on application though Habeas Corpus and prohibition were available to subjects from very early time. The term ' Prerogative writ' shows that it is specifically associated with the King. Thus, these writs of Habeas Corpus etc. were so called because they had their origin in the exercise of the King's prerogative, as the 'fountain of justice', to superintend the due observance of the law by his officials and tribunals. Originally they were issued by the King's Bench only at the instance of the crown and by means of these writs the crown compelled the subordinate authorities to carry out their duties properly, so that no subjects was injured by the act of any public authority which could not be justified by law.

In England Royal prerogatives were assigned to any natural man but King was personified as corporation sole and thus these 'prerogative writs' were also assigned to it. Thus these writs, were issued from king-in-council. With the developments of Common Law Courts of the King's Bench which was emanated from Curia Regis (Royal Council) assumed more responsibility.

The King's Bench had at its command a number of special writs - the so called 'Prerogative writs' - by the issue of which it could control the activities of inferior authorities throughout the realm, This jurisdiction no doubt was there due to prerogative of the crown. During the twelvth and thirteenth centuries these writs assumed the form of an administrative

---

1. Blackstone's Comm. (iii), C.18.
2. History of English Courts, by Maitland, P. 25.

order to inferior authorities and its own officers. According to Coke "The Court had jurisdiction over its own officials" and in certain cases.

"This court may hold plea by a Bill without any writ in Chancery as for, or against any officer, minister, or privileged person of this court." Thus the court had a general superintendence over the due observance of law by officials and administrative bodies. This supervisory jurisdiction used to be exercised by means of prerogative writs which were conceived 'flowing from the king himself, sitting in his (King's Bench) courts, superintending the police and preserving the peace of country."

During the fourteenth century, the court of King's Bench gradually became a separate court of Common Law as it lost its former close connection with the King himself. But while thus becoming simply Common Law Court, it preserved both in its style and its jurisdiction traces of the days when it was a court of a very different King. It retained powers of a quasi-political nature which came to it from the days when the court held Coramrege was both King's Bench and Council.[3]

Blackstone in his well known commentaries[4] describes the King's Bench "as the remnant of aularegia" and refers to the justices of King's Bench.

"Who are by their office the sovereign conservators of the peace and supreme coroners of the lend."

This passage and its context derive from the fourth part of Coke's Institute where the highest language is used concerning the justices of the King's Bench:

"It is truly said that the justices de banco regin have supreme authority. the King himself sitting there as the law intends. It is therefore. not surprising that its authority to exercise a supervisory powerover all other authorities was at no time questioned."

---

3. Holsworth History of English Law, Vol.1(4th Ed.)p. 211.
4. Rd, 1765-9, 5th Ed. 1773: See book III Chap. IV. p. 41.

When, during the fourteenth century, the court of King's Bench, became a truly judicial body it could still exercise control over various administrative bodies although it could not interfere directly with their discretionary governmental powers. The notion then prevailing was that any person or body which exercised jurisdiction, that is to say which had the power to determine and decide something, was a court subject to the supervisory jurisdiction of the King's Bench. The widest statement of the rule, and one very frequently quoted is to be found in the judgement of the court of King's Bench delivered by Holt, C.J. in Rex vs. Inhabitants of Glamorganshire (1700):[5]

"The court will examine the proceedings of all jurisdiction erected by Act of Parliament."

This point is brought out by the manner in which the King's Bench controlled the activities of the justice of the Peace and the Commissioners of Sewers.

The office of the justice of the Peace goes back over six centuries - to the statute of 1 Edw. 3, State-2, C.10, - passed in the year 1327 which provided that 'for the better keeping and maintenance of the peace, the king will see that in every country goodmen and lawful, which be in the country, shall be assigned to keep peace'. Originally the duties of a justice were similar to that of a constable - to arrest suspects and to see that they were held in custody until they could take the trial. Afterwards the minor offences such as drunkenness, swearing and vagrancy began to be tried by the justices summarily. Gradually they acquired power to hear and determine felonies and misdemeanours. Their court, which came to be known as 'Quarter Sessions' was to be held four times a year. In the exercise of their jurisdiction at Quarter sessions, the justices were under control of King's Bench. The prerogative writs were used by the court to compel the justices to act when they ought to act but refused to do so and to quash the convictions given by them beyond their jurisdiction. This feature of control exercised by the King's Bench is not so striking as the control wielded by the court over the

---

5. 1 Ld. Raym (1700)

administrative duties of the justices. As the time passed, the justices of the peace came to be known as the 'men of all work' of the administration.

These justices were regarded as exercising 'Jurisdiction' at all times whether performing purely judicial or administrative functions, in or out sessions. Of course the justices and their 'courts' were subject to the control of the King's Bench through prerogative writs.

Maitland puts this point well while speaking of the justices of the Peace as:

"We puzzle foreigners by our lay use of the word 'Jurisdiction' and it is remarkable enough. What ever the justices has had to do has soon become the exercise of a jurisdiction. whether he was refusing a license or sentencing a thief. this was an exercise of jurisdiction, an application of the law to a particular case. "[6]

Commissioners of Sewers

The Sewer Commissioners were entrusted with the work of maintaining the sea walls at various places on all sides of the coast of England. It was the statute of 1532 which vested in the commissioners the power to survey the "walls, ditches, gutters, sewers, bridges," and also to find out who was responsible for keeping them unrepaired, to arrange workmen for repairs and to make "necessary and convenient ordinances and statutes for safety of the said sea-coasts and neighbouring parts" as well as marshes. The later statutes also conferred upon the commissioners the power to sell the land by giving good title to the purchaser in case the landowners failed to pay the assessed charges. Soon after it was found that various projects undertaken by the Commissioners came into conflict with the rights of the landholders and this gave rise to a direct conflict of the Commissioners with the landowners. It was found between 1610 to 1616 that taxes were levied on the towns, land and chattels by

---

6. Maitland - The Shallows and Silences of Real Life Collected papers. Vol. I, at p. 478.

the Commissioners for assessments which remained unpaid. If there were errors on the face of the orders of the Commissioners, the court of King's Bench used to quash such orders such as when the Commissioners failed to set out the necessary facts to show that they had jurisdiction in the matter.

In Hently V. Boyer[7], the Commissioners were fined and imprisoned for acting illegally. As a prohibitory measure against this King of act the King's Council, issued an order whereby the interference with the Sewer Commissioners was forbidden and at the same time declared that the court had no authority to review the validity of administrative projects. During the period the court of Star Chamber existed, the Sewer Commissioners including different administrative bodies were effectively controlled by it and the exclusion of the King's Bench did not make much difference. But after the abolition of Star Chamber, the exercise of their administrative functions were again passed under the supervision of the King's Bench. It is in the case of Cummins V. Massam[8] that the judges of the King's Bench Division claimed their authority over the Sewer Commissioners and to quash their orders issued a prerogative writ of certiorare. The control thus exercised over the Commissioners of Sewers was used by Holt C.J., as a precedent to control the order of any tribunal set up by Parliament. This type of function was progressively extended unless the -court of the King's Bench, which had its monopoly in issuing prerogative writs, became, a Supreme Court of administration, supervising much of the business of Local Government by keeping subordinate bodies within their legal limitations by writs of certiorari and prohibition, and ordering them to perform their duties by writ of mandamus. The modern High Court had succeeded to much of this jurisdiction, and there can be no doubt that the absence in the common law system of a distinct body of public law, whereby proceedings against public authorities are instituted only before special administrative courts and are governed by a special body

---

7. (1615) 79 English Reports, 287
8. 8 82 E.R. 473 (1642). 8 82 E.R. 473 (1642).

of rules, is directly traceable to the extensive use of prerogative writs by the Court of King's Bench. [9]

In R. V. Electricity Commissioners,[10] which is a landmark in the History of writs, Atkin. L.J. said : "Whenever any body of persons having legal authority to determine questions affecting the rights of subjects and having the duty to act judicially, act in excess of their legal authority, they are subject to the controlling jurisdiction of the King's Bench Division, exercised in these writs." He then has fully illustrated by examples indicating therein how certiorari and prohibition have been issued in different cases by different courts and he has reached the conclusion that both certiorari and prohibition would be applicable to the determinations of the Electricity Commissioners under the Electricity Act.

It has thus been seen that these writs of Habeas Corpus, Certiorari, prohibition, mandamus and Quowaranto were called prerogative writs because they had their origin in the exercise of King's prerogative, as the 'fountain of justice'. to superinted the due observance of the law by his officials and tribunals. Originally they were issued by the King's Bench only that the instance of the crown and by means of these writs the Crown compelled the subordinate authorities to carry out their duties properly, so that no subject was injured by the act of any public authority which could not be justified by law. Since the eighteenth century, the writs came to be issued also at the instance of private persons, but the original characteristics of the writs were maintained, namely, that they were issued by the High Court in the King's name, to control inferior courts, tribunals or other public authorities. The special characteristic of a prerogative writ was procedural. A rule nisi was issued expert, on the application for the writ on behalf of the agreed party, calling upon the opposite party why the rule nisi should not be made absolute, and, then on hearing the opposite party, the court

---

9. "The prerogative writs" (1951) Cambridge Law Journal, pp. 55-56.
10. (1924) 1 K.B. 171.

would either discharge the rule nisi or make it absolute and issue the writ prayed for.[11]

(B) HISTORY OF WRITS IN ENGLISH LAW

After the Norman Conquest the Central administration grew very strong. The Common Law within certain limits, during the Middle Ages, could restrain the Central administration. During the thirteenth century when the judicature and the executive have become distinct from each other, a common law applicable to the entire nation was administered by the King's judges in the Royal Courts. Under the Tudor period there was high ascendancy of the Royal power yet the Tudor Monarchs adhered to the traditional policy that the King, although not under any man, ruled under God and law. During the first half of the thirteenth century Bracton, in his famous book on English Law, held this doctrine reiterating the fact that the rulers and the ruled both were equally bound by the law and deserved justice according to law. As is evident from the year Books the Common lawyers of the subsequent two centuries i.e. fourteenth and fifteenth, also accepted this view.

It is observed that the doctrine enunciated by Bracton received application by the Courts in various ways during the period Henry IV and **Elezabeth I reigned. Darey V. Alein"**[12] a decision of the King's Bench in 1602, during the closing years of Elezabeth I's reign, is a good illustration. The grantee, among other things had been given the sole right of making playing cards for a period of years within the English realm but the court held it against the common law and hence void.

The only period when this conception of the rule of law was seriously questioned was the Stuart period. The Stuart King's questioned the conception of the rule of law thinking that the Royal prerogative, which was the sovereign power, could override the legal provisions when they deemed fit. This opens a direct conflict between the Stuart King's and the judges regarding their right to determine aspects touching the Royal prerogative.

---

11. Home Secretary V.O. Barien (1923) L.J.K.B. 830 (1923) A.C. 603.
12. 11 Co. Rep. 84-B.

In the beginning of the seventeenth century i.e. in 1612, Bacon in his essay entitled 'Judicature' declared that the judges should be 'Lions', but under the throne' He specifically stated, "it is a happy thing in a State when King and States do often consult with judges, and again, when judges do often consult with King and States; the one when there is matter of law intervenient in business of states; the other, when there is some consideration of State intervenient in matter of law".

The views of Lord Chief Justice Coke were, however, diametrically opposed to that of Bacon. Only because Coke stressed on the supremacy of law he was later dismissed from the Bench. These circumstances invoked the attention of James I who once 'Harangued' the judges asserting that the judges were duty bound to respect the Royal prerogative.

'**First**', said the King,

"encroach not upon the prerogative of the Crown; if there falls out a question that concerns my prerogative or mystery of State, deal not with it, till you consult with the King, or his council, or both; for they are transcendent matters...."

'Secondly',

"that you keep yourselves within your own Benches. not to invade other jurisdictions, which is unfit and unlawful things, Keep you therefore all in your own bounds, and for my part, I desire you to give no more right, in my private prerogative, than you give to any subject, and therein I will be acquiescent : as for the absolute prerogative of the crown, that is no subject for the tongue of a lawyer, nor is lawful to be disputed."

James on a subsequent occasion called the judges and advised them that it was his outlook to decide the forum of a case. Cook's account of the audience is as follows :

"Then the King said that he thought that the law was founded upon reason, and that he and others had reasons as well as the judges : to which it was answered by me that, true it was, that God had endowed His Majesty with excellent science and great endowments of nature; but His Majesty was not learned in the laws of his realm of England and causes which concern the life or inheritance, or goods, or fortunes of his subjects, are not to be decided by natural reason, but by the artificial reason and judgement of law, which law is an art which requires long study and experience, before that a man can attain to the cognizance of it; and that the law was the golden netwand and measure to try the causes to the subjects; and which protected His Majesty in safety and peace: with which the King was greatly offended, and said that then he should be under the law, which was treason to affirm, as he said; to which I said, that Bracton said quad Hexnon debate case sub homine.[13]

In the seventeenth century struggle which took place later in between the King and Parliament, the judges and the lawyers made common cause with Parliament against the King. For this reason, the revolution of 1688 has been called "the triumph of lawyers over the executive. Two essential features of the settlement were that the independence of the judges was established on firmer ground. Henceforth the executive could not rely on any inherent powers other than those defined and limited prerogatives of the crown.

"The conflict between King and commons died out with the development of constitutional monarchy and Cabinet Government, but the conflict between James and his Judges it survived long afterwards in a antagonism between the legal procession and the Executive."[14]

It is now a well established fact that the executive should not interfere with the judiciary in the exercise of its judicial function but the converse is not true because whenever it is alleged that a Minister or a Department or any official has acted unlawfully, the judiciary does interfere with the executive. In France uniquely enough the principle of separation of powers is held to mean that each of the three branches, i.e. the legislature, the executive, and the judiciary, of the Government shall be self-contained without any interference with the other. Thus the ordinary courts in France are not empowered to enquire into the

---

13. Prohibition Del Roy (1607) 12 Co. Rep. 63.
14. Trevelyan, History of England 506

legality of administrative decisions to avoid any interference with the executive branch of the Government. From it this follows that an appeal from administrative authority lies to the higher administrative authority just as an appeal from a judicial court lies to a higher court. In England the concept of the rule of law implied that the judiciary, including even ordinary courts, should have powers to enquire into the legality of executive acts.

The concept of the rule of law means that the executive is not above the law, and what it does must he done in the due exercise of the powers conferred by law upon it Of course Parliament, being supreme, can arm executive with extraordinary powers, and apart from such statutory powers, the Crown has under law certain rights which are not shared by ordinary people. Accordingly the executive and the courts remain subject to the provisions of the law. If the ordinary courts cannot intervene in the executive sphere, it is attributable to non-provision of the law and not to the executive being inaccessible.

(C) HISTORY OF WRITS IN INDIA,

On the establishment of a Supreme Court in 1774. at Fort William in Bengal, under the Statute 13. George III, Chapter 63, commonly know as Regulating Act, 1773, the History of writs in India may be said to have ushered in.

The Royal Charter'"[15] establishing the Supreme Court"[16] at Calcutta was issued by King George III on March 26, 1774. The Charter under clause five conferred upon the Supreme Court all the powers and privileges of the Courts of King's Bench in England and this undoubtedly meant the authority of the Supreme Court also in respect of issuing prerogative writs. The Supreme Court was also a court of record as per provisions made in clause four of the Charter. It was a King's Court and not a Company's Court. Its judges were appointed by British Crown and not by the Company or the Governor General. Sir Flijah

---

15. It is supposed to have been drafted by Sir Elijah Impey.
16. The first Judge of Supreme Court landed in Calcutta on 19th November 1774.

Impey, a Barrister from England, was appointed first Chief Justice of this court.[17]

The Supreme Court, under Clause 21 of the Charter had supervisory jurisdiction over the court of requests and court of Quarter Session and the justices, sheriffs and magistrates employed under the previous Charter. Clause 21 of the Charter provided that the aforesaid courts and authorities :

"Shall be subject to the order and control of the said Supreme Court of Judicature, at Fort William in Bengal, in such sort, manner and form, as the inferior courts and magistrates at, and in that part of the Great Britain called England are, by Law, subject to the order and control of our Court of King's Bench; to which end, the said Supreme Court of Judicature at Fort William in Bengal is hereby empowered and authorised, to award and issue a write of writs of mandamus, certiorari, procedendo, or error, to be prepared in manner above mentioned, and directed to such courts or magistrates as the case may require, and to punish any contempt of wilful disobedience there unto by fines and imprisonment."

Thus, Clause 21 cited above explicitly conferred upon the Supreme Court the power of issuing writs of mandamus, certiorari, procedendo and error to the courts of Requests. the court of Quarter Session and Justices, Sheriffs and other magistrates referred to therein, Of course there are diverse opinions on the point that the justices of the Supreme Courts were to issue only these four writs as mentioned above and to the two Courts and officers mentioned in Clause 21"[18] but it is an established fact without any doubt that the Supreme Court did issue prerogative writs. This power to issue these prerogative writs may be said to flow from the terms of Clause 4, which confers on the Chief Justice or justices severally and respectively.

---

17. Harihar Prasad Dubey - 'A short history of the Judicial Systems of India and some Foreign Countries', 1968. p.106.
18. See M.P. Jain. Indian Legal History, pp. 117-119.

"such jurisdiction and authority as our justices of our own court of King's Bench have, and lawfully exercise within that part of Great Britain called, England, by the Common Law thereof."

Accordingly under these provisions the Supreme Court could issue any of the prerogative writs throughout Bengal, Bihar and Orissa and against any British subject or servants of the company.

The Supreme Court was purposely established for exercising supervision and control over the administration of the East India. It is historical fact that subsequently there was a strong cleavage and conflict between the judges of the Supreme Court and executive Government headed by Governor-General in Council. The court issued prerogative writs to the executive Government i.e. the officers of the East Indian Company in respect of their official acts. As sequel to this in consequence of the proceedings in Patna"[19] and Cassijurah"[20] cases the Governor-General in Council employed military forces to impede orders of the court being carried out. The Parliament wanted to introduce the English principle of judicial review in India but the Company's Government in India had different views. The executive authorities of the company submitted a petition to the authorities in England against the efforts made by the Supreme Court in India to introduce the English Law to the inhabitants of Bengal and Bihar and to remedy this obstacle the statute of 1781 "[21] was issued.

The main purpose of the Act so passed was to explain and amend the Act of 1773,

"and for the relief of certain persons imprisoned at Calcutta under a judgment of the Supreme Court, and also for

---

19. Patna case-Fifth report in East India Affairs (1917) (Reprint) Vol. 1 CCLXXI. In this case the Supreme Court gave judgment with heavy damages against the officers of Patna Provincial Council in their judicial capacity. For detailed discussion see M.P. Jain "Legal History" at 139-142.
20. Fifth report on East India Affairs (1917) Vol. CCLXVI - for detail see M.P.Jain "Legal History" pp. 139-142.
21. 21 Gee. III, C. 70.

indemnifying the Governor-General and Council and all officers who have acted under their orders or authority in the undue resistance made to the process of the Supreme Court".

It was stated in it that the Act of 1773 and the Charter which had been issued under it had created doubts and difficulties and that,

"by reason thereof dissensions hath arisen between the judges and the Governor-General and Council."

In Section I of the Act it was provided that the Governor-General and Council 'should not be subject to the jurisdiction of the Supreme Court for or by reason of any act or order or any other matter of thing whatsoever counseled or ordered or done by them in their public capacity only'. The Act provided that the questions of inheritance or contract were beyond its jurisdiction and no land holder or former of land or land rent, was subject to court's jurisdiction irrespective of the fact of their being employed by the company or by a British subject. It was of course open to the Supreme Court to try cases for wrongs and trespasses or other civil cases submitted thereto by agreement in writing. In brief, the jurisdiction of the Supreme Court was curtailed only to the original civil jurisdiction of a territorial nature over all persons within the town of Calcutta, and a personal jurisdiction over British subjects, i.e. European subjects, outside such territorial limits, but within what may be roughly called the presidency of Bengal, but such personal jurisdiction was confined to actions for wrongs and trespasses.

(D) WRIT JURISDICTION OF COURTS IN INDIA
Writ jurisdiction after 1781

The Act of 1781 as noted above curtailed the jurisdiction of the Supreme Court to the Presidency town of Calcutta, In view of the modification of jurisdiction, it seems clear that the Supreme Court could not issue a prerogative writ beyond the Presidency town of Calcutta except in special cases where the party happened to be a British subject or Company's servant who had voluntarily consented to submit to its jurisdiction even though beyond the territorial limit of the town. Though there has been some conflict of judicial opinion with respect to the Supreme Courts power to issue writs"[22] beyond Calcutta, but Privy Council in Ryots of Garabhandho V. Zamindar of Parlakimedi'[23] authoritatively decided that the Supreme Court after 1781 did not claim or exercise jurisdiction of issuing English prerogative writs of mandamus and certiorari over the Country courts in Bengal and Bihar. Their Lordships of the Privy Council observed :

"It would be a task of some difficulty and little profit to investigate the practice before 1781, but their Lordships are not satisfied.... that either of these writs was employed at all, though Habeas Corpus was certainly employed. However that may be, their Lordships think it reasonably plain that between 1781 and the end of the centuryno such jurisdiction was being exercised in fact. They know of no cases in which the Supreme Court issued either certiorari or mandnus to a country court. The writ of Habeas Corpus came to be used in the form ad testifican dum - that is a mode of summoning witness - in the course of the Supreme Court's admitted jurisdiction over Calcutta and over British subjects.... Whether the writ ad subjiciendum was issued beyond the local jurisdiction only to British subjects, or to others for the purpose of protecting the liberty of British subjects. or more generally in aid of the Court's local jurisdiction within Calcutta - in a question to which the answer is not altogether clear. But this writ would not ordinarily, if ever, issue to a court, and their Lordships know of no case after 1781 until the Bombay case of 1829 (In re-Justices of the Supreme Court of Judicature at Bombay) in which this writ was used by any of the supreme Courts so as to interfere with the jurisdiction of any court of the company. It would seem probable that the exercise of such jurisdiction would have produced a definite reaction on the part of the council and that such a jurisdiction would have been constantly appealed to by litigants unsuccessful in the Country Courts."[24]

---

22. In re : Nataraja Iyer. 16 Indian Cases (1912).
23. A.I.R. (1943) P.C. 164.

These well know historical facts put here, prove that before this the prerogative writs were issued in India to a very limited extent.

Writ Jurisdiction of Supreme Courts of Madras and Bombay :

Madras,

The British Parliament passed an Act in 1800 whereby the crown was authorized to abolish the Recorder's Court at Madras and instead establish a Supreme Court. The charter under this Act was granted in December 1801. The new court"[25] was given the same powers and had the same restrictions and limitations as the Supreme Court of Calcutta.

Bombay

The Supreme Court of Bombay was established in 1823 under statute 3 George IV, C. 71 and it was mentioned in clause 7 'that it shall be lawful for his Majesty to establish a Supreme Court at Bombay to be invested with such powers and authorities and privileges, restrictions and control as the said Supreme Court of Judicature of Fort- William in Bengal by virtue of any law, now in force.... is invested or subject to.......

The Supreme Courts of Madras and Bombay had similar powers to issue the prerogative writs, under their respective charters as that of Supreme Court of Calcutta with the difference that the Calcutta Court could issue writs beyond the local limits of its jurisdiction, whereas these courts (Madras and Bombay) had no such power. These three Supreme Courts of Judicature functioned till 1861-62 when they were replaced by the Calcutta, Madras and Bombay High Courts respectively, created under the Indian High Courts Act, 1861 (25 and 25 vict, C 104).[26]

High Courts Act 1861 :

---

24. Per Viscount Simon L.C. in Ryots of Garbandho V. Zamidar of Parlakimedi, A.I.R. (1943) p.c. 164-170.
25. Clause 8 of Charter 1801.
26. H.P.Dubey - 'A short History of the Judicial Systems of India and some Foreign Countries, 1968' p. 149.

Upto 1861 in the Provinces of Bengal, Bombay and Madras two parallel judicial systems were operating. One set of courts consisted of the Supreme Courts of Judicature, representing the Crown, and which functioned in the Presidency towns where Europeans and Englishmen mostly resided; and the other set of courts, established by the company, functioned in the Presidency of the Provinces. It was in 1858 that the Government of India was put under the direct control of the crown. Thus under the changed situations after 1858 the difference and distinction between the Company's Courts and the Crown's courts had disappeared. The High Court's Act of 1861 amalgamated the two sets of courts into one at the Presidency towns of Calcutta, Bombay and Madras and under the provisions of the Act the Crown was given the power to set up, by letters patent, High Courts of Judicature in Calcutta, Madras and Bombay, and with the emergence of these High Courts the old chartered Supreme Courts and the Company's Courts were to be abolished, and the jurisdiction and powers of the abolished courts were to be transferred to the new High Courts.[27] Under the Act power was given to establish other High Courts with the same constitution and powers as the ones set up at Presidency town.[28] Writ Jurisdiction of High Courts : Before the present constitution (1950) came into force the three charted High Courts of Calcutta, Madras and Bombay

only were vested with the power of issuing writs of certiorari and prohibition and such jurisdiction was limited to the ordinary original civil jurisdiction of the High Courts on the territorial basis i.e. the jurisdiction of the High Courts in the Presidency towns was confined to the limits of their original jurisdiction, as a result of which they could not issue the writs to persons or tribunals residing or situated outside the Presidency towns.[29] The High Courts derived the powers of issuing such

---

27. The letters patent with respect to these three High Courts bear date December 28, 1865.
28. Under this power a High Courts was established at Allahabad in 1867, at Patna in 1916. at Nagpur and Assam in 1948.
29. Nomani V. Banwari Lal (1947) 51 C.W.N. (P.C.) and Mathew V. Distt.

writs within their territorial jurisdiction as successor of the Supreme Courts which had been exercising jurisdiction over the Presidency towns of Calcutta, Madras and Bombay and were replaced by the High Courts. They had also the jurisdiction to issue writs in the nature of mandamus but the territorial jurisdiction was similarly restricted. Under section 491 of the Criminal Procedure Code the High Courts were also empowered to issue writs in the nature of Habeas-Corpus through out the whole province under their respective jurisdiction. Except these High Courts others had no power to issue the prerogative writs save the writ of Habeas Corpus i.e. the power to issue the prerogative writs was restricted only to the High Court in the three Presidency towns other High Courts had no such jurisdiction.[30]

Thus these three High Courts were given all the powers and jurisdiction of the erstwhile Supreme Courts and Company Court. But as mentioned above the Supreme Courts had no power of superintendence over courts and officers exercising jurisdiction beyond the limits of the Presidency towns. Under section 15 of the High Court Act these new High Courts were given the power of superintendence over all the courts which were subject to their appellate jurisdiction throughout the territorial limits of the High Court. But no power of superintendence was Conferred over such persons and authorities which were not designated as courts and happened to be situated outside the Presidency towns, nor even over courts which were not subject to the appellate jurisdiction of the High Courts. The Presidency High Courts established under the High Court Act 1861 or under subsequent legislative enactments were not given the power of issuing prerogative writs because there were no Supreme Courts exercising the power of superintendence by means of prerogative writs in their cases as had been in the cases of the Presidency High Courts.

Magistrate of Trivendrum (1939) 43. C.W.N. 981 (P.0).
30. Ryotes of Garabhandho V.Zamindar of Parlakimedi,A I R.(1943) p.c. 164.

Enlargement of the Jurisdiction under the new Constitution,

Before the commencement of the new Constitution the position of writs was a indicated here-under :

1) The power of issuing writs was conferred upon only to the three Presidency High Courts and not to other High Courts.
2) The High Courts in the Presidency towns had limited jurisdiction in respect of their original civil jurisdiction.

Consequently they were devoid of any power to issue writs to the tribunals or persons beyond the three Presidency Towns.

Under Article 226 not only the power of the three Presidency High Courts is extended in matter of issuing writs but all High Courts in India have a similar power of issuing writs which bring in a uniformity in the power of High Courts for issuing writs. The object of the framers of our Constitution in adopting Article 226 was to remove all the limitations mentioned earlier and to place all the High Courts in the territory of India in the same situation as the High Courts of England in the matter of the power to issue writs, and in same respect, even in a better position. The purpose of granting such-power to the High Courts by the makers of the Constitution has been explained by the Supreme Courts in Election Commission V. Saka Venkata Rao[31] :

"In that situation, the makers of the Constitution, having decided to provide for certain basic safeguards for the people in the new set up, which they called fundamental rights, evidently thought it necessary to provide also a quick and inexpensive remedy for the enforcement of such rights and, finding that the prerogative writs, which the courts in England has developed and used whenever urgency demanded immediate and decisive interposition, were peculiarly suited for the purpose, they conferred, in the State's sphere, new and wide powers on the High Court of issuing directions, orders, or writs primarily for the enforcement of fundamental rights, the power to issue such directions. etc 'for any other purpose' being also included with a

---

31. A.I.R. (1953) S.C. 210; (1953) S.C.R. 1144 at 1150.

view apparently to place all the High Courts in this country in somewhat the same position as the court of King's Bench in England."

This writ jurisdiction extend to all authorities, persons and also Government falling within the jurisdiction of each High Court. Under Fifteenth Amendment to the Constitution the High Courts are empowered to issue directions, orders or writs to any authority or Government even if that authority or Government is situated beyond their territorial jurisdiction provided the cause of action arose within the jurisdiction of the respective High Courts.

Articles 32 and 226 are very wide and do not fetter the powers of the Supreme Court and the High Courts in respect of issuing prerogative writs as is seen with regard to the prerogative writs in English Law even then it has been held that the broad and basic principles regulating the issue of writs under the English Law should be followed by the courts in India. The point has been illustrated elaborately by Mukerji, J, in a unanimous judgement in T.C. Bassappa V. T. Naggappa : [32]

"In view of the express provision in our constitution we need not now look back to the early history or the procedural technicalities of these writs in English Law, not feel oppressed by any difference or change of opinion expressed by particular cases by English judges. We can make an order or issue a writ in nature of certiorari in all appropriate cases and in appropriate manner, as long as we keep to the broad and fundamental principles that regulate the exercise of jurisdiction in the matter of granting such writs in English Law.[33] In this way it is clear that to a considerable extent the principles of English Law regarding the prerogative writs are followed in India. Of course some Indian

---

32. A.I.R. (1954) S.C. 440.
33. Also observed the Banarjee, J., of Calcutta High Court in Union of India V. Elbridge Watson, A.I.R. (1952) Cal. 601 "constitution had adopted the nomenclature of the English Writs and I apprehend the English Law relating to these writs must govern the issue of the writs here in so far as they are not opposed to our constitution" at p. 603.

High Courts were prone on departing from the principles showing their desire to review findings of the fact of inferior tribunal in writ proceedings but the Supreme Court of India vide Parry and Co. Ltd., Dare House, Madras V. Commercial Employees Association, Madras'[34] and Veerappa Pillai V. Raman and Raman Ltd.[35] has held that status quo he maintained. In another case of Hari Vishnu Karmath V. Syed Ahmed[36] and others the Supreme Court declared that a court will not review findings of fact of inferior court or tribunal. Here the Indian position is parallel to that of the English-practice that a superior court does not go into review of findings of the fact[37]. This particular aspect is taken here to illustrate the tendency of courts and in later Chapter nature, scope and grounds of certiorari will be discussed and there it will be seen that Indian Courts have practically followed the principles of English Law Governing certiorari.

---

34. A.I.R. 1952 S.C. 179.
35. A.I.R. 1952 S.C. 192.
36. A.I.R. (1955) S.C. 233.
37. See S.A. De Smith 'Judicial Review of Administrative Action' Chapter III.

2 Chapter

ORIGIN, HISTORY AND NATURE OF CERTIORARI

(A) HISTORY OF CERTIORARI
(i) IN ENGLAND

Histrologically certiorari was issued to bring the records of an inferior code into the King's Bench for review or to remove indictment for trial in that court in England, the writ of certiorari is of great antiquity forming part of the process by which the King's Court restrained court of inferior jurisdiction from exceeding their powers. In origin"[38] certiorari was a royal demand for information; the kingwishing to be certified of some matter ordered that the necessary information to be provided for him. The Register of writs (1227) and Elacitorium Abbreviation C. Henry III contain numerous writs of certiorari issued for a wide diversity of purpose. But the information in such cases was, as a general rules provided by sending the relevant documents and specially those documents known as "records". The Register of writs gives many examples. Thus, certiorari lay to order the return of securities of the peace, recognisance,[39] statutes merchant and stable.[40] Sometimes by means of this writ, the judgement of inferior court was alleged to be incomplete, certiorari issued to order the remainder of the record to be

---

38. The old writ of certiorari was abolished by the Administration of Justice (Miscellaneous Provisions) Act 1938 and it is replaced by new or for certiorari, having the same effect, but with different procedure.
39. An acknowledgement of debt owing to the Crown enrolled in a court with a condition to be void on the performance of thing stipulated
40. A land of record under the seal of the debtors authenticated by the royal seal; execution of which was immediate.

returned. The Treasurer and Chamberlains if Excchequere were ordered on certiorari to find out whether a manner was held in ancient demesne. In medieval times certiorari was, therefore, granted for a number of purposes other than review. In brief, the following were some of purposes served by certiorari :

1) To inquire with allegations of extortion made by His Majesty's subjects.[41]
2) To make inquisitions.[42]
3) To remove a case to the King's Bench before a trial or judgement, where King's interest was involved.[43]
4) To obtain a record from one court for use in a suit in another.[44]
5) To obtain execution against property of the different situated in other country.[45]
6) To obtain information for administrative purposes; e.g. where sherif ordered to find out the where abouts of a person who had been granted King's protection.[46]

During Edward III reign, certiorari was often used to remove indictment into the King's Bench and upon their removal the King would proceed to prosecute in his own court. In the Fifteenth and Sixteenth centuries, the trail of indictments was removed by certiorari constituted an important part of King's Bench work.

From about 1280 the writ was in common use in judicial proceedings e.g. the conception then prevailing was that Sovereign had been appealed to by some one of his subjects who complained of an injustice done to him in an inferior court, 'whereupon the Sovereign saying that he wished to be certified - certiorari of the matter ordered that the record etc, be transmitted into court where he was sitting,[47] i.e. King's Bench

---

41. Placitorium Abbreviations, 155 (49 Hanry Ill); Commissioners were appointed to inquire into the allegations.
42. Register of original writs.
43. Place : Abbr. 182, r.14 (56 Hanry Ill).
44. Register of writs.
45. S.ed. Soc. Vol. 57, 41 (1291)
46. Stephen, History of Criminal Law, 1, 96.

Court. in order that the court should do what was necessary to be done in the interest of justice. This might be a trait in better qualified court, whether the King's Bench or elsewhere, it might be more efficient from of execution, e.g., in that wider sphere where the King's Bench waits ran; it might be in order that after judgement a pardon should be granted by the King; it might be that the proceedings ought to be corrected or quashed.

Certionari in Old English Treaties

Sir Anthony Fittz - Herbert (1470-1538) in the New Natura Brevium, with the commentary ascribed to Sir Mathew Hale, says : "Certiorari is an original writ,[48] sometimes out of Chancery and sanctioned out of King's Bench, and where the King would be certified of any record which is in the treasury or in the common pleas, or in any other court of record or before the Sherrif and Coroners. or of a record before Commissioners or before the cascheator, he may send his writs to any of the said court or offices to certify such records before him in banco or in Chancery". Numerous forms of the writs are subjoined, to judges itinerant, coroners, judges of goal delivery, Sherrifs, or to bishop to certify a list of ineumbents since the time of Edward IV. Then Bacon's Abridgment,[49] under the title 'certiorari' says "A certiorari is an original writ issuing out of chancery or the King's Bench, in the King's name directed to the judges or officers of (a) inferior courts, commanding them to return the records of proceeding of some cause in action pending before them, to the end of the party may have more sure and speedy justice before him or such other justice as he shall assign to determine the cause". Again at page 13(h) : The courts of chancery and King's Bench may award a certiorari to remove the proceeding from any inferior courts, whether they be of any ancient or newly created jurisdiction, unless the statute or charter, which creates them,

---

47. V. Titchmarsh (1915) 22 Dominion L.R. 272, 277.
48. The technical distinction between 'original' and 'judicial' writs is that while former issued out of chancery (not the court but office. the latter issued out of the court in which the proceedings had begun.
49. Vol. 47th Pd. p.9.

exempts them from such jurisdiction." Viner's Abridgment Vol. IV"[50] title, "Certiorari (a) out of what court it ought to issue" to whom; at a contra "If the record be pleaded in more base court that in which it is, the court may grant a certiorari". Comyn's Digest Vol. II,[51] Title, "Certiorari" follows Fitz-Herbert, and gives numerous instances where certiorari is issued, e.g. one of the censers of the college of Physicians to remove a judgement by them for malpractices and "so to every inferior jurisdiction of record, though it be within the country platine or inwales". Lily's Practical Register"[52] gives this description. Certiorari is a writ which issues out of the King's Bench to inferior courts commanding them to certify to them the loquela, viz. the plaint, which when returned, then upon a rule given bail must be put in before a judge or else a writ procendando will be granted.

(B) DEVELOPMENT OF CERTIORARI IN ENGLAND

The bodies and persons subject to control by certiorari:

In order to understand the development of certiorari, we must examine here the bodies subject and exempted from the control of certiorari.

(i) Inferior Courts"[53]: In earlier times the majority of cases concerned inferior courts such a magistrates courts and country courts. For this reason. Twentieth century book describes the writ of certiorari as "a writ issuing from the Crown side of the King's Bench Division of the High Court of justice, directed to the justice of the peace, or judges of inferior courts; requiring them to certify to that court of some conviction, order of session, order of justices. or other matter of judicial nature depending upon them, in order that the same may be dispensed with there in such manner as the court shall think fit.[54] Instances of different

---

50. (1748) 1415.
51. (1822)
52. (1735) Vol. p. 365
53. An inferior court is one which can be stopped from exceeding its jurisdiction by a writ of prohibition issuing from the superior court. Secondly, it must appear in its proceeding that court was acting within its jurisdiction, whereas a proceeding of a superior court it will be presumed that it acted within its jurisdiction

inferior courts to which certiorari is issued at one time or another are countless and include court merchant,[55] the court of Admirality[56] and the courts of Forest.[57]

(ii) Justice of Peace : As early as in Edward III's time the court of King's Bench supervised the session of the peace by issuing certiorari to remove before all unfurnished indictments lying before the justices in the country it was visiting.[58] The power to issue certiorari to justices has always existed,[59] but cases of its application are now comparatively rare on account of justices Protection Act, 1848,[60] The Summary Judicature Act, 1848"[61] and Summary Jurisdiction Act.[62]

Bodies exempt from Certiorari

(1) Ecclesiatical Courts : In R.V. Chancellor of St. Edmundsbury and Ipswich Diocese"[63] it was held that certiorari does not lie to an ecclesistical court, then the fact of such court being subject to prohibition was no proof of their inferior rank, and that the ecclesiastical courts were not inferior courts. Wrottesley and Evershed L. JJ, in court of appeal also affirmed that certiorari does not lie to an ecclesiatical court. In his judgement Wrottesley L. J., quoted Ricketts V. Bodenham"[64] in which Lettledale J. interrupted Sir Fredrick Pollok to say : "Those are cases of common law courts, which are inferior to the courts of Westminister Hall; but ecclesiastical courts are not so"[65] Again at

---

54. Archhold's Quarter Sessions (1908) p.127.
55. Select cases concerning the law merchant Vol. I-Ill (Seld. Soc. Vol. 23,. p. 46.
56. Select pleas in the court of Admirality (Seld Soc. Vol. 6). 2
57. Nelson in the English Government at work, 1327-36
58. Putman, Proceedings before the Justices of the Peace in the 14th and 15th Century, CXX.
59. R. V. yarpale (1790) 4 T.Q.R. 71, R. Glomorganshire (1793).
60. This Act placed limitations on these actions.
61. This Act standardised the form of conviction so all the mention of the evidence or the reasoning by which the justices reached their decision omitted.
62. This Act instituted the modern form of the case stated.
63. (1947) K.B. 263 (1948) 1 K.B., 195, 197.
64. (1836) 4 A&E 433, 446.
65. Ibid.

page 204, Wrollesley L.J. said'[66] "The order of certiorari is modern substitute for the old writ of certiorari, and the researches of all concerned have failed to discover any case of writ of certiorari issuing to an ecclesiastical court to bring up and quash any proceedings. Writs of certiorari have issued to bishops, calling upon them to certify the common law courts, on the chancery, matters peculiarly within the knowledge of bishops, such as list of incumbents in a parish, whether a person who has pleaded benefit of allergy in criminal case is in fact a clerk, and so forth"[67]

(2) Arbitrators: There is no instance in the Law Reports when certiorari has gone to any arbitrators except a statutory arbitrator. In R.V. National Joint Council for the Graft of Dental Technicians (Dispute Committee), ex-parte Neate.[68] Lord Goddard said "I have never heard of certiorari or prohibition going to an arbitrator. and in this respect I am going to apply to this matter the words of Lord Summer in the well known case of Admirality Commissioner V. S.S. Amerika.[69] There the question was whether an action lay for the death of a person, and he said : "never in the many centuries that have passed since reports of the decisions of English courts first began has the recovery of damages for the death of a human being as a civil injury has been recorded". I should apply that to this case, and say that never during the many centuries that have passed since reports of the decisions of English court first began is there any trace of any arbitrator being controlled by this court by writ of prohibition or certiorari."

Similarly Denning L.J. in his historical survey in Northumberland"[70] case said that in arbitrators awards the King's Bench never interfered by certiorari, because a private tribunal, not subject to certiorari was concerned.[71] We have seen

---

66. Ibid.
67. See Gordon"Certiorari to Ecclesiastical court" 63 LQR (1947) 208.
68. (1953) 1 K.B. 705, 707.
69. (1917) A.C. 38, 51.
70. (1952) 1 K.B. 338, 351
71. If the arbitrator was guilty of misconduct a motion to set aside

in the above brief sketch of historical facts that from the later years of Henery III reign until the end of the 16th Century writ of certiorari issued for great variety of purposes.[72] From 1600 onwards writ issued for quashing the orders and convictions by inferior courts for irregularity. Just at this time the court of King's Bench began to exercise control over commissioners of sewers,[73] officials responsible at that time for the care of ditches and waterways irrigating lands in their district. The court of King's Bench used writ of certiorari to quash the orders of commissioners for errors on " face of them.[74] In Groenvelt V. Burnwell,[75] it was held that the writ would issue to review disciplinary decisions of the errors of College of Physicians, Lord Holt in this case said : "....... for it is a consequence of all jurisdiction, to have them proceedings returned here..... where any court is erected by statute, a certiorari lies to it .... which may command them to send their proceedings before them that it may be seen whether they confine themselves to their jurisdiction, which if they, this court may correct them......" Again ......" And the court is to examine, as far as appears on record, that they have not exceeded their authority, and if they have not, and not pursued the Act, to quash proceedings."

In 18th century most administrative powers were in the hand, of justice of peace and whatever the justices had to do was controllable by the prerogative writs. No distinction was made between judicial and administrative powers. Then to quote Bankes L.J. "As statutory bodies were brought into existence exercising legal jurisdiction, so the issue of the writ come to be extended to such bodies. There are numerous instances in the books commencing in the quite early times".

---

award could be obtained : Kent V. Elastob (1802) 3 East 18.
72. See S.A.deSmith"The prerogative writs" (1951)11 Camb.L.J.40. 45.
73. Commissioners were set up by statute in 1532. For anaccount of Commissioners of Sewers, see Holdswroth, "History of English Law" Vol. X. pp 199-206.
74. Cummins V. Massan (1643) Chilly's Practice Vol. III, 370.
75. (1700) XXX 1 Ld. Raym 454.

"In case of R.V. Inhabitants of Glamorganshire (1700) Ld. Raym 580,[76] the court expressed the general opinion that it would examine the proceedings of all jurisdictions erected by Act of Patent........."

When in 19th Century administrative powers were mostly transferred to new authorities, the judges continued to grant certiorari to review their administrative functions. A series of decisions laid down that the acts of a local authority such as Board of Health or Board of Works could be reviewed in much the same way as the Act of justice. Other types of cases in which certiorari issued,[77] rent and rate matters,[78] Overseer's cases,[79] Surveyor's cases.[80] tax cases,[81] highway cases"[82] and title cases.[83]

Hence it is important to remember that the King's Bench which exercised control over the administrative functions of the justices by means of prerogative writs of certiorari and mandamus has continued to exercise such control over their successors, the modern local and central government authorities. Ultimately, the question whether the writ of certiorari would issue in a particular case came to be determined by reference to the character of the act that was impinged rather than by reference to the character of the body that had authority to do something. If the act or decision in question was of a judicial character it was amenable to certiorari. No longer was the availability of the writ limited to courts stricto sense or even to bodies closely resembling courts. The traditional formalities of the administration of justice may be entirely absent. As *Serulton L.J. once said in the Court of Appear*[84] - "when speaking of what that it should be a court in the sense in which this court is a court, it was enough if it is exercising, after hearing evidence, judicial

---

76. R. V. Poor Law Commissioners 1 Jur. N.S. 251.
77. Arthur V. Commissioners of Sewers of Yorkshire(1724) 8 Mod. 331.
78. R. V. Harman (1793) Andr. 343.
79. Walsall Overseers V. L.N.W.R. (1878) 4 A.C. 30.
80. R. V. West Riding of Yorkshire JJ (1794) 5 T.R.629
81. R. V. Cann (1746) 2 Stra, 1263.
82. R. V. Jauntal St. Mary's (1815) 3 M & S. 465,
83. Thorpe V. Cooper (1828) 2 Y & I 445.
84. R. V. London Country Council (1931) 2 K.B. 215, 233.

functions in the sense that it has to decide on evidence between a proposal and opposition....."

Thus, historically prohibition was a read whereby the royal courts of common law prohibited other courts from intertraining matters failing within the exlusive jurisdiction of common law courts. Cerctiorari was issued to bring the record of an inferior court into the King's Bench for review or to remove indictments for trial in that court. Mandamus was directed to inferior courts and tribunals and to public officers and bodies to order the performance of a public duty. All three were called progrative writs. They are discratrionary reads but the principles for issuing such writs are well settled.[85]

(C) HISTORY AND DEVELOPMENT OF CERTIORARI IN INDIA (Pre 1950 Position)

In India jurisdiction exercised by a High Court in matter of certiorari was original supervisory and corrective, thus, broadly speaking, English principles governing the certiorari were applied by the High Courts and certiorari could be issued against inferior tribunals and statutory bodies to see whether they properly exercised their jurisdiction.[86] In Ryots of Garabando V. Zamindar of Parlkimod[87] Viscount Simon observed : "....... The ancient writ of certiorari in England is an original writ which may issue out of a superior court requiring that a record of the proceeding in some cause or matter pending before an inferior tribunal should be transmitted into the superior court to be there dealt with. The writ is so named because in its original Latin form it required that the King should "be certified" of the proceedings to be investigated, and the object is to secure by the exercise of the authority of a superior court, that the jurisdiction of the inferior tribunal should be properly exercised.

The writ of certiorari was first introduced in India in 1773 under the provision of Regulating Act, 1773 when the first court empowered to issue writ was the Supreme Court at

---

85. Halsbury's large of England fourth Ed. (Re.Issue) Vol. I Para 103.
86. Venkta Raman V. Secretary of State 1930 Madras 896.
87. A.I.R. 1943, P.C. 164.

Calcutta established by Royal Charter"[88] in 1774. Similarly clause 8 of the Charter of 1800 and Clause 10 of Charter of 1823 empowered the Supreme Court in Madras and Bombay respectively to issue writ of certiorari. When Supreme Courts were replaced by High Courts under the Indian High Courts Act, 1861 the Presidency High Courts of Calcutta, Madras and Bombay were also give the power to issue the writ. The jurisdiction for the operation of the writ was confined to the original jurisdiction of the respective High Courts.

The earliest Bombay case where writ of certiorari was granted to remove a case from the Court of Small causes to the High Courts was Pirbhai Khinji V. B. Baroda and Central Indian Railway Company"[89] and the earliest Madras case when the writ of certiorari was issued by the High Court independent of its jurisdiction over the Presidency lawn was *Penugonda Venkataratnam V. Secretory of State of India.*[90] The effect of this was that in whole of India certiorari ran only within three Presidency Towns till January 26. 1950. However, the Rangoon High Court in the first case"[91] that came before it for writ of certiorari held that it had jurisdiction to issue that writ either under the inherent powers or under express statuary provisions. The **Patna High Court in Gopal Marwari V. King Emperor**"[92] and the Nagpur High Court in **D.V. Bapat V. Registrar Co-operative Societies**"[93] held that they had no jurisdiction to issue writ of certiorari. This position continued till present constitution came into existence.

Certiorari Under the Present India Constitution

The present Constitution of India introduced notable changes with regard to the issue of writs. Certain rights, civil in nature, have been enshrined in the Constitution of India as 'fundamental rights'. For enforcing these fundamental rights the

---

88. Clause 21 Read with Clause 4.
89. (1871) Born. H.C.R.P. 59.
90. A.I.R. (1930) Mad, p. 896.
91. In Re Maung Pyu, I.L.R. (1940) Rang. p. 325.
92. (1943) 209 I.C. p. 482.
93. I.L.R. (1941) Nag. p. 392.

Constitution empowers the Supreme Court and all High Courts to issue direction, orders and writs including writs in the nature of Habeas Corpus, mandamus, prohibition, quo-warranto and certiorari, which ever may be appropriate. Thus evidently the issue of writs by the Supreme Court and the High Courts is also in the nature of a remedy for enforcing the fundamental rights. In this regards the High Courts have however, been assigned an enlarged jurisdiction for the issue of writs, beside enforcing 'fundamental rights' for any other purpose as well.

Undoubtedly, this is a very substantial advance upon the position that existed before the Constitution of"[94] 1950. Articles 32 and 226 of the Constitution empower these courts"[95] to issue the writs not only in the restrictive sense of prerogative writs but even over a wide field. They can issue any direction or orders or even some other form of writ to any person or authority including in appropriate cases any Government. Thus, Article 32 and 226 have enabled the Supreme Court and the High Courts to control to some extent administrative authorities in the modern administrative era. It may be submitted that the provisions made under Article 226 where by the High Courts have been empowered to issue writs which may be in the nature of remedy for enforcing fundamental rights or for any other purpose, are not derogative of the power conferred upon the Supreme Court in India by Clause (2) of Article 32. Thus, in the preconstitutional era the jurisdiction to issue the prerogative reads was enjoyed only by three chartered High Courts of Bombay. Calcutta and Madras in India but with the comming into force of the constitution all the High Courts and the Supreme Court are conferred powers to issue the prerogative including the writ of certiorari under Article 226 at Article 32 of the constitution respectively.

---

94. Seatalvod, The Common Law in India at p. 197 (Hamlyn) Lectures, 1960.
95. Supreme Court and High Courts

(D) NATURE OF CERTIORARI

The writ of certiorari, in an order, directed to an inferior tribunal, requiring the record of the proceeding in some cause or matter to be transmitted into the superior court to be dealt with there. In modern practice, the most important aspect of the writ is in its use as a means of controlling inferior courts and other persons and bodies having legal authority to determine the rights of citizens and having the duty to act judicially. As observed by Goddard C.J. in R. V. Metropolitan Police Commissioners"[96] "that in recent years with the development of administrative law under which government departments are given wide powers of holding enquiries and then making orders which may affect of the property and persons, the remedy of certiorari has been considerably extended." Where no right of appeal to the court exists, this writ as well as other prerogative writs are the principal means by which the determination of tribunals can be brought before the courts. The degrees of control which can, however, he exercised is necessarily a limited one.

The writ is in the nature of immediate remedy. It is a means of obtaining a speedy decision as to the jurisdiction of public bodies, including government departments. The importance of the writ lies in the fact that since it is a prerogative writ it can be sought for by an aggrieved party without first bringing any suit or proceeding ordinarily one must first file a suit before one can get any kind of order from the court whether the order in the nature of certiorari or mandamus or any other kind of order. But so far as the prerogative writs are concerned, one can straight-away go to the court and apply for the appropriate writ without filling any suit or proceeding Thus certiorari is an extra-ordinary legal remedy and is corrective in nature issued by superior court to the inferior tribunal etc. Which deals with civil rights of persons as a public authority.[97]

Certiorari lies only in respect of judicial acts[98]

---

96. (1953) 2 All R R 717.
97. V.G. Ramchandran, "Low of Writs", p. 397.
98. 61 Judicial acts implies quasi judicial acts - Board of Education V.

The rule is that any body of persons having legal authority to determine question affecting the rights of citizens, and having the duty to act judicially, is subject to the controlling jurisdiction of the superior courts exercised by means of prohibition and certiorari. It is not necessary that is should be a court - an administrative body in ascertaining facts or law may be under a duty to act judicially notwithstanding that its proceedings have none of the formalities of, are not in accordance with the practice of a court of law. A body may be under a duty to act judicially although there is no form of lis inter parts before it it is enough that it should have to determine a question solely on the facts of the particular case, solely on the evidence before, apart from question of policy or any other extraneous consideration.

R. V. Manchester Legal Aid Committee[99]

Moreover, an administrative body, whose decision in whole or in part is arrived at by considerations of policy may be under a duty to act judicially in the course of arriving at that decision. Thus, if, in order to arrive at the decision, the body concerned had to consider proposals and objections and consider evidence, from the stage of initiating the proceedings leading upto the decision, there was something in the nature of a lis before it, then in the course of such consideration and at that stage the body would be under a duty to act judicially.

If, on the other hand, an administrative body in arriving at its decision has before it at one stage any form of lis and throughout has to consider the question from the point of view of policy and expediency, it cannot be said that it is under a duty at any time to act judicially unless the duty to act judicially is imposed by the statute conferring power on the body to decide a particular matter. Even where the body is at some stage of the proceeding leading upto the decision under a duty to act judicially, the supervisory jurisdiction of the court does not extend to considering the sufficiency of the grounds for or

---

Rice (1911) A.C.P. 179.
99. (1952) 1 All E R 480.

otherwise challenging the decision itself.6 And according to a recent decision 'duty to act judicially' would to determined from the nature of power possessed by administrative authority.[100]

(A) PROHIBITION AND CERTIORARI [101]

Originally, prohibition was aimed at forbidding inferior courts to continue proceedings in excess of jurisdiction, while certiorari required the records of proceedings or orders of inferior courts to be brought up so that, amongst other purposes, the decision might be quashed if found defective on certain grounds which included want of jurisdiction, bias by interest, a failure to observe the rules of natural justice and of error of law. Both these remedies have been brought into the realm of administrative law, and there the value of certiorari is far greater than prohibition except that the use of prohibition in this field is generally determined by the time at which the aid of the courts is sought. If the decision has not been reached, prohibition is the proper procedure : but once it is given the appropriate remedy is certiorari.

Thus, a writ of certiorari to call for regards and examine. The same for passing appropriate order is issued by a superior court to an inferior court which certify its records for examination. Certiorari lies to bring decision of an inferior court, tribunal, public authority are any other body of persons before the superior courts for review so that the court may determine whether they should be quashed or to quash such decisions. The order of prohibition is an order issuing out of superior court and directed an inferior court are tribunal or public authority which forbids that court or tribunal or public authority not to act in excess of its jurisdiction or contrary to law. Both certiorari and prohibition are employed for the control of inferior courts, tribunals and public authorities, the difference is only of stage of issue.

---

100. Robinson V. Minister of Town and Country Planning (1947) K.B. p. 717.
101. Ridge V. Baldwin (1964) A.G. 40.

3 Chapter

SCOPE OF CERTIORARI

(A) INTRODUCTORY

The scope of certiorari is mainly confined to acts of judicial or quasi judicial nature and generally does not embrace the purely inistrative decisions. The reason for this limitation is a historical one. We have seen that certiorari started as a means of correcting usurpation or abuses of judicial power and though it has spread into the administrative sphere, it has never got away from its connections with judicial function. The whole foundation of certiorari is therefore vests upon the distinction between judicial acts and administrative acts. In view of this it is clearly of fundamental importance to determine the meaning of the terms judicial and quasi judicial on the threshold of our inquiry we are faced with the problem of slemarratinn and difficulty what does not constitute the judicial element that will permit of challenge by certiorari. There is no simple solution of this difficulty and the courts are still in the process of working in out. As Allen has observed "once again is asking to determine what is "judicial" authority, the riddle of administrative or judicial strips mockingly at us. The utmost variation exists in the means of case law.[1] The difficulties encountered desire mainly from constitutional importance of maintaining, not an absolute, but a substantial separation of judicial executive powers.

It is familiar law that certiorari and prohibition will only issue where the power sought to be controlled are judicial or quasi-judicial in nature. The famous dictum of Lord Atkin in R. V. Electricity Commissioner[2] where he observed "whenever any

---

1. Sir C.K. Allen 'Law and Order' 3rd Edition (1965) at p.221.
2. (1924) 1 K.B. p. 171, which has been described as 'The Classic

body of persons having legal authority to determine question affecting the rights of subjects and having the duty to act judicially act in excess of their legal authority they are subject to the controlling jurisdiction of King's Bench Decision exercised in these writs" (emphasis added) serves the starting point of modern law. This has been quoted over and over again in connection with the definition of 'quasi-judicial' is English and Indian cases. In view of this limitation in the use of certiorari, it is clearly of fundamental importance to determine the meaning of terms 'judicial' and 'quasi- judicial'.

(B) WHAT IS JUDICIAL

The Donoughmore Committee on Ministers powers in report at P.73 states that a true judicial decision presupposes an existing dispute between two or more parties. and then involves four requisites;

1) the presentation of their case by the parties to the dispute;
2) if the dispute between them is a question of fact, the ascertainment of the fact often with the assistance of argument by or on behalf of the parties on evidence;
3) if the dispute between them is a question of law, the submission of legal arguments by the parties and,
4) a decision which disposes of whole matter by a finding upon the facts in dispute and application of the law of land to the facts so found, including where required a ruling upon any disputed question of law.

Further the most exhaustive description of judicial function is to be found in Shell Company of BP Australia Ltd. V. Federal Commissioner of Taxation.[3] The question in issue was whether the Board of Review which had been set up in 1925 under the Commonwealth Income Tax Legislation was a court exercising the judicial power of the Commonwealth. If so. certain

---

statement which serves as the starting point for modern law comes from case of 1923. S.N. Shukla 'Judicial Control of Administrative Process'(1967) at p. 309. a

3. (1965) 112 C.L.R. 386.

limitations concerning the tenure of office of the Board members might have been unconstitutional. The High Court of Australia decided by a majority that it was an administrative and not a judicial tribunal and this majority judgment was affirmed in appeal by Privy-Council. Lord Sankey remarked in the course of his judgement that "the authorities are clear to show that there are tribunals with many of a trappings of a courts which, ever the less, are not courts in thestrie sense of exercising judicial power " Mere externals do not make a direction to an administrative officer by an adhoc tribunal an exercise be a court of judicial power. The actual decision in the case rested on the ground that the Board of Review could not be a judicial tribunal as its order were not conclusive for any purpose whatsoever. The decision it seems has only a negative values the Lord Chancellor enumerated a series of negative propositions which stated, inter alia, that a tribunal is not necessarily a court because two or more contending parties appear before it, nor because it have witness or give a final decision which affects the right of parties. The judgment quoted with approval certain assertion of Griffith CJ, given in another Australian case, namely, Huddart Parker and Co.Pvt. Ltd. V. Moorhead"[4] which to some extend neutralised the effect of the negative tests own irritated in the judgment. The observation of Griffth C.J. regarding judicial powers are a follows" the power which every saveraigh authority must of necessity have to decide controvaries between its subjects or between itself and its subjects and whether the rights relate to life, liberty or property. The exercise of this power does not begin until some treatment which has power to give a binding and authoritative decision (whether subject to appeal or not) is called upon to take action.

In Huddant Parker's case, Isacs J., referred to the statement of Palles C.B. in E.V.L.G.B. Irelands[5] ...." to a tribunal into a court, ... so as to make is that its determination judicial, the essential should have by its determination within jurisdiction... to

---
4. (1909) 8 C.L.R., 330.
5. 5 (1902) 2 I.R. p. - 349, 375.

impose liability or effect rights." "By this, " said, the learned chief Baren, "I mean that the liability is imposed or rights by the determination only, and not by the fact determined, and so that the liability will exist, or the right will be affected, although the determination may be wrong in law or in facts". To same up on this case, the definition given by Griffith C.J. of judicial power was approved, and that definition limits the impression to tribunals with power to binding judgment. The one obvious criticism of this reasoning is that it first paints out that the essence of judicial power is the power to make a binding decision but at the same time a tribunal possessing this power is not necessarily a court or authority wielding judicial power.

The next case, Labour Relations Board of Saskatchevva V. John East Iron Works[6], in this case we get another fundamental test which distinguishes a judicial body from an administrative body, namely, that the former decide controversies according to law. The question in issue was whether the Labour Relations Board exercise judicial power; and if so, whether in that exercise it is analogous to a country court. The Judicial Committee of Privy Council decided in negative. Lord Simond, delivering the judgment of the Privy Council, said; The borderland in which judicial and administrative functions overlap is a wide one ... Without attempting to give a comprehensive definition of judicial power, they accept the view that its broad features are accurately stated in that part of the judgment of Griffith C.J. in Huddart, Parker & Co. Pvt. Ltd. V. Moorhead case which was approved by this Board in Shell Company V. Federal Commissioner. Nor do they doubt, as was pointed out in the latter case. that there are many positive features which are essential to the existence of judicial power, yet by themselves are not conclusive of it. or that any combination of such feature will fail to establish a judicial power it, as is a common characteristic of so-called administrative tribunals. the ultimate decision may be determined not merely by the application of legal principles to certain facts but by consideration of policy also. Whether in the

---

6. (1949) A.G. 134.

present case the power, exercised by the appellant Board is a judicial power, their Lordships do not decide. For the elements in its constitution and functions which at least make it doubtful whether it is in the strickt sense a court exercising judicial power at all appear to lead conclusively to the opinion that it is not a superior, district or county court or a court analogous there to.... It is a truism that the conception of the judicial function is inseparably bound up with the idea of a suit between parties, whether between crown and subject or between subject and subject; and that it is the duty of the court to decide the issue between these parties, with whom alone it rests to initiate or defend or compromise the proceedings."

This approach identifies the judicial power with the application of legal principles and excludes adjudication based on consideration of policy. It is well known that cases, like Talf Vals case[7] " Sorrel V. Smitt,[8] and Snail in the Bottle case"[9] were decided by the House of Lords on consideration of policy. Moreover, the observations of Lord Simonds, quoted above, in connection with the functions of Labour Board seen to suggest that the judicial power can only be exercised by courts and not by administrative bodies. It must be conceded that the courts in India1[10]" and England[11]" have not been able to formulate a satisfactory definition of a judicial proceeding. Sometime they have characterised as judicial. The same is in the United States. In the States of Alababna, Massachusettsa and Michigan, the courts have held that the actions of the commissioners of highways or of a city council is laying out highways and streets is judicial. In Maine and New Hampshire, on the other hand, this same act has been held as being of a nonjudicial character. If the cases are analysed it comes to no more that this; that if the judges want to interfere they say that a decision has the element of being judicial

---

7. Toff Vale Rly. V. Amalgamated Society of Rly. Senants (1900) A.C. 426.
8. (1925) A.C. 700.
9. Donoghue V. Stevenson (1932) A.C. 562.
10. See... XXN S.N. Shukla "Judicial Control of Administrative process".
11. See .... H.W. R. Wade, "Administrative Law".

and if they do not want to interfere, they say that the decision is ministerial.

Inspite of these difficulties we are now in a position to suggest the primary characteristic of judicial functions, by whomsoever exercised. But it may be emphasized that the resence and absence of any of these characteristics, does not furnish any conclusive test whether a particular body is judicial body or not. The characteristics of the judical function thus are :

a) The power to hear and determine a controversy between two or more parties.
b) (be5tre) The power to make a binding decision which may affect persons or property or other rights of the parties involved in the dispute.
c) The decisions with regard to rights and liabilities is arrived at by giving an opportunity to the party who is to be affected by an order to make representation, making some kind of inquiry, hearing and weighing evidence, if any, and considering all the facts and contents bearing on merits of a controversy.[12]
d) The power to make a binding decision involves no exercise of discretion.[13] It is one which disposes of the case by a finding upon the facts in dispute and an application of the law of the land to facts so found. (e) The power to make a binding decision is exercised at
e) the request of a person interested.

(C) ADMINISTRATIVE DECISIONS

Administrative action it is difficult to define the terms `administrative action'. It includes all the three elements of governmental powers : legislation, adjudication and execution. It may be briefly said that administrative action is that which is

---

12. A Judicial inquiry investigates, de on present or past fact and un clares, and enforces liabilities as they stand der law supposed already to exists, that its purpose and end. Justice.
13. This seems to be implied in the fourth requisite of a pure judicial decision according to report of Minister's Powers.

performed by an administrative body. Administrative action is the action of and administrative organ and an administrative organ is a part of that branch of the state engaged in public administration outside the ordinary Judicature and Legislature. Administrative organ is stronger than the other branches of state organs and in times of great emergency it alone may function. Purely administrative decisions stand apart from the judicial decisions. In the former, the Minister or his Department or some official there in, acts throughout in a discretionary manner which usually reflects or implements some matter of policy. As the Committee on Ministers Powers put it in their report "In the case of administrative decision there is no legal obligation upon the person charged with the duty of reaching the decision to consider and weight submissions and arguments, or to collect any evidence, or to solve any issue. The grounds upon which he acts, and he means which he takes to inform himself before acting, are left entirely to his discretion."

The following are main characteristic of an administrative functions :

a) A valid administrative act presupposes the existence of a legal authority in the officer or department to do that act.
b) Such acts in many cases affect the rights of citizens.
c) The administrative decision turns ultimately on discretion.

In other words, the administrator is entitled to arrive at his decision by reference to considerations of policy. The judges or a tribunal performing the judicial function of applying an existing legal rule to the facts as found by him is in a different position from the administrator. Again, it may be the duty of the administrator to exercise his discretion in initiating action. The judge or a tribunal must await a dispute coming before it, then it can function at all.

(D) QUASI-JUDICIAL DECISIONS

But in between the judicial and the administrative decisions, and exhibiting some of the characteristics of each, is what the Committee on Minister's Power called the quasi-judicial decision. A judicial decision, as noted by the Committee, implies the presentation of their case by the parties to the dispute, the ascertainment of the relevant facts and application of the relevant law to the relevant findings of facts. A quasi-judicial decision to connotes a dispute and the ascertainment of the facts; but the decision is not, as in the case of a judicial decision, simply a matter of applying the law to the facts. It involves the exercise of ministerial discretion. As the Committee put it... the minister has to make up his mind whether he will or will not take administrative action and if so what action. His ultimate decision is 'quasi-judicial' and not judicial, because it is governed, not by a statutory direction to him to apply the law of the land to the facts and act accordingly, but by a statutory permission to use his discretion after he has ascertained the facts and to be guided by considerations of public policy. It is a decision which in its final-phase 'ultimately turn on administrative policy'.

One of the most familiar examples to a quasi-judicial function is the power of a minister to confirm a local authority's slum clearance scheme under the Housing Acts. The confirmation by a minister must frequently be proceeded by a public inquiry by an official appointed by the minister. The holding of inquiry involves the hearing of evidence, and this resembles the judicial process. The decision involves the exercise of discretion; the minister must take into account the findings of the inquiry.

Thus the minister, while to some degree acting as a judge arrives at his decision not by applying the fixed rules of law, but by exercise of his own judgment as to what in the circumstances is fair and just; "Though the act of affirming a clearance order is administrative act, the consideration which must proceed the doing of that act is of a quasi-judicial consideration [14] Another example of this type of decision is the power of the minister to confirm the compulsory purchase of land by a local authority for such purposes as housing, education, the construction of roads or the development of land. Before the decision can be properly taken, facts have to be ascertained and private interests, if they are likely to be affected, to be considered. It is this preliminary

---

14. Errington V. Minister of Health (1935) 1 K.B. 249, 273.

stage which is quasi-judicial. But after this inquiry stage ended then minister do not act in quasi-judicial capacity"[15] and his decision is an administrative act. [16]

The Committee on Minister's Powers drew a fairly sharp line between judicial and quasi-judicial functions in some of their recommendations; they regarded the latter functions, as noted above, as primarily administrative. But critic have shown that the distinction drawn is too obscure to offer reliable guidelines. The difficulty in the way of doing so is two-fold. First, as Dr. Robson points out in his Justice and *Administrative Law*[17],' the dividing line is by no means sharp and clear; the judicial function may involves a discretionary decision just as the administrative function may, on occasion, becomes in essence judicial. And. secondly, the quasi-judicial function covers an extremely wide range of decision, run ranging from what is all but judicial to what is all but administrative. Nevertheless. despite all these criticisms, as Professor Robson himself indicates"[18] lawyers have to decide, in practical cases arising in the courts, whether a particular activity was of a judicial or an administrative character because prohibition and certiorari will lie in respect of judicial acts and not for those of an administrative or ministerial character, and therefore distinction continue to be drawn by courts. The pamphlet of conservative society has also made certain observations on the recommendation of Committee on Minister's powers, "But their distinctions between quasi-judicial and Administrative decisions, i.e. the pre-existence of a dispute is not one to which we can subscribe. For the type of decision in any given class of case is the same whether or not there is a dispute. Further. a dispute as a rightness of decision may arise only after the Minister has made it an can hardly he said them to change respectively the nature of decision." [19]

---

15. Franklin V. Minister of Town and Counting Planning (1948) A.C. 87.
16. 16 See -H.W.R. Wade,'Towards Administrative Justice' pp.65-67.
17. 3rd Edition, (1951) 444.
18. Ibid, p.51
19. Rule of Law - A study by the gums of court of conservation and Unionist Society – 195. 5 at p. 34.

It can be said that it is perfectly true that it is impossible to observe any one rule which will enable us to distinguish judicial and quasi-judicial act on one hand and judicial and administrative on the other hand. It is submitted that the courts have been influenced by the consequences of calling a function judicial, quasi-judicial or administrative, and those consequences vary from case to case. Yet if the dividing line between these functions is hard to find, it is at least possible to point out certain essentials that will do the decision under consideration with the essential elements of a decision of a judicial character with a question " The expression is sadly laying in precision". [20]

Essential Elements :

(1) Act of a competent authority imposing liability on or affecting rights of others. In Reg. V. Dublin Corporation[21] the question raised was whether a borough rate levied by a corporation was illegal or not. It was found that the borough fund of corporation.... was otherwise insufficient by reason of certain illegal payments made out by it. To make up the deficiency, the corporation levied a borough rate. The legality of which was challenged and writ of certiorari was prayed to quash all the orders and resolution of the corporation in connection with the imposition of the rate. The writ was granted and May C.J. while discussing the meaning of 'judicial act' observed as follows :

It has been contended in this case that no certiorari can issue to remove the borough rate, and this point must be first considered. It is established that the writ of certiorari does not lie to remove and adjudicate the validity of judicial acts. In this connection the them 'judicial does not necessarily mean acts of judge or legal tribunal sitting for the determination of matters of law, but for purpose of this question a judicial act seems to be an act done by competent authority, upon consideration of facts and circumstances, and imposing liability or affecting rights of others. An if there by a body empowered by law to inquire into facts,

---

20. As observed by Lord Somorbell of Harrow in Vine V. National Dock Board (1957) A.C. 488.
21. 2 L. R. 371

make estimates to impose involving such consequences would be judicial acts."

This definition was approved by Palles C.B. in Re Local Government board[22] and was described by Lord Atkin in Erome United Breweries Co. Ltd. V. Bath justices[23] as an of the best definition of judicial act as distinguished from an administrative act.

(A) DUTY TO ACT JUDICIALLY

The R. V. Electricity Commissioners[24], Atkin L.J. said; "Whenever any body of persons having legal authority to determine question affecting the rights of subjects, and having the duty to act judicially, act in excess of their legal authority they are subject to the controlling jurisdiction of king's Bench Division exercised in these writs". This has been described as a classic dictum which serves starting point for modern law.[25] The observation has been constantly repeated and approved in many English and Indian decisions upto this day. In King V. London Count Council[26] Slesser L.J., in his judgment analysed these conditions Atkin L.J. in above case as follows "Atkin L.J. as he then was in the case of R.V. Electricity Commissioner, lays down four conditions in which it is appropriate that certiorari should issue. He said, whenever any body of person 'firstly' 'having legal authority secondly' to determine question affecting the rights of subjects and thirdly having the duty to act judically fourthly act in excess of their legal authority. The subdivisions. I need hardly say, are my aim they are subject to controlling jurisdiction of king's Bench Division In R. V. Legislative Church Assembly[27] Lord Hewart said : "In order that a body may satisfy the required test, it is not enough that it should have legal authority to determine question affecting the rights of subjects, there must be superadded to that characteristic a further characteristic that a

---

22. (1885) 16 L.R. 150.
23. (1926) A.C. 586.
24. (1924) 1 K.B. 171.
25. S.N. Shukla, "Judicial Control of Administrative Process" p. 309.
26. (1931) 2 K.B. 215.
27. (1928) 1 K.B. 411..

body has a duty to act judicially (emphasis added). Here we see that the scope of judicial decision was narrowed down.

In Nakkuda Ali V. Jayratne,[28] the judicial Committee of the Privy Council reaffirmed above test and noted: "... the basis of the jurisdiction of the courts by way of certiorari has been so exhaustively analysed in recent years that individual instances are new only of importance as illustrating a general principle that is beyond dispute. The principle is most precisely stated in the words of Atkin L.J. (as he then was) in Rex V. Electricity Commissioner " After citing passages from Electricity Commissioner's case and the Church Assembly case noted above, their Lordship concluded that unless there was a duty to act judicially the mere authority to determine questions affecting rights does not amount to a judicial act' when he cancels a license he is not determining a question; he is taking executive action to withdraw a privilege " (emphasis added).

But in a recent leading case of Ridge V. Baldwin,[29] Lord Reid made certain absentions regarding 'judicial' element of an act. Lord Reid accepted Lord Atkin's dictum as noted above in Electricity commission's case as most authoritative but he criticised Lord Hewart C.J.'s dictum (noted above) and he calls it a glass on definition of Atkin L.J. Lord Reid also disapproved Nakuda Ali's case and emphasised that in R.V. Electricity Commissioners, Lord Atkin was prepared to infer a judicial element from the nature of power alone, After quoting dictum of Lord Hewed, Lord Reid observed • " If Lord Hewart meant that it never enough that a body simply has duty to determine what the rights of an individual should be, but that there always something more to impose on it a duty to act judicially before it can be found to observe the principles of natural justices, then not appears to me impossible with earlier authority " Again observed :

"There is not a word in Lord Atkin's judgment to suggest disapproval the earlier line of authority which I have cited on the contrary, he goes further than those authorities I have already

---

28. (1951) A.C. 66
29. (1964) A.G. 40

stated my views that it is more difficult to courts to control in exercise of power on a large scale where treatment to be noted out to a particular individual is only one of matters to be considered. This was a case of that kind, and if Lord Atkin was prepared to infer a judicial element from the nature of power in this case he could hardly disapprove of a particular individual."

Lord Reid also demolished the Nakkuda Ali's ruling on this point. After a careful analysis of Nakkuda Ali's case he observed, "of course, if it were right to that Lord Hewart's glass or Lord Atkin stated "a general principle that is beyond dispute" the rest would follow. But I have given my reasons for holding that it does no such thing, and in my judgment the older cases do not "illustrate" any such general principle-they contradict it. No case older that 1911 was cited in Nakkuda Ali's case on this question, and question was only one of several questions which were argued and decided. So I am forced to the conclusions that this part of judgment in Nakkuda's case was given under a serious misapprehension of the effect of the old authorities and therefore cannot be regarded as authoritative."

Indian Cases

The starting point of modern law on this question is the case of Province of Bombay V. Khusal Das Advani.[30] The Indian Supreme Court discussed at length the meaning of term of judicial and quasi judicial. In this case Kania C.J. who spoke for majority discussed with approval the May C.J. dictum in R. V. Dubbin Corporation also approved the dictum of Atkin C.J. or the four condition analysed by Slesser L.J[31] He observes : "The respondent's argument that whenever there is a determination of a fact which affects the right of parties, the decision is quasi-judicial, does not appear to me sound. The observations of May C.J., when properly read, included the judicial aspect of determination in the words used by him. I am led to that conclusion because after the test of judicial duty of the body making the decision was expressly stated and emphasized by

---

30. 30 A.I.R.(1950) S.C. 222.
31. pp. 224-226 - Paras 5,6,7

Atkin's Slesser L.J. in no subsequent decision it is even suggested that the dictum of May C.J. was different from the statement of law of the two Lord Justices or that the latter, in any way required to be modified. The word "quasi-judicial" itself necessarily implies the existence of the judicial element in the process leading to the decision. Indeed, in the judgment of the lower court, while it is stated at one place that if the act done by the inferior body is a judicial act, as distinguished from a ministerial act. certiorari will lie, a little later the idea has got mixed up where it is broadly stated that when the fact has to be determined by an objective test and when that decision affects rights of someone, the decision or act is quasi-judicial. This last statement overlooks the aspect that every decision of the executive generally is a decision of fact and in most cases affects the right of some one or this other. Because an executive authority has to determine certain objective facts as a preliminary step to the discharge of an extensive functions, it does not follow that it must determine those facts)udicial)y. When the executive authority has to form an opinion about an objective matter as a preliminary state the exercise of a certain power conferred on it, the determination of the objective fact and the exercise of the power based thereon are alike matters of an administrative character and are not amenable to the writ of certiorari.

In the same case Das J., concurred with the view that even on the footing that the decision as to public purpose was an objective one, it did not necessarily become a quasi-judicial decision. He made the following observations:

"Thus a person entrusted to do an administrative act has often to determine question of fact to enable him to exercise his power. He has to consider facts and circumstances and to weigh pros and cons in his mind before he makes up his mind to exercise his power just as a person exercising a judicial or quasi-judicial function has to do. Both have to act in good faith. A good and valid administrative act binds the subject and affects his rights or imposes liability on him just as effectively as a quasi-judicial act does. The exercise of an administrative or executive act may well be and is frequently made dependent by the legislature upon a condition or contingency which may involve a question of fact, but the question of fulfillment of which may; nevertheless, be left to the subjective opinion or satisfaction of the executive authority, as was done in the several ordinances.

Regulations and enactments considered and construed in the several caused referred to above. The first two items of the definition given by Atkin L.J. may be equally applicable to an administrative act. The real test which distinguishes a quasi-judicial act from an administrative act is the third item in Atkin L.J. & definition, namely, the duty to act judicially." (at p. 257).

According to the majority view in Khusal Das's case, two conditions are essential, inter alia, to constitute a decision as a quasi-judicial one, namely, first, the decision must be an objective one; second, there must be over and above this, a 'duty to act judicially'.

According to the minority judgments in the above case Mukherjee and Mahajan JJ the duty to decide objectively imports the idea of a quasi-judicial function. Mukherjee J. observed :

"There is a well-marked distinction between forming a personal or private opinion about a matter and determining it judicially. In the performance of an executive act, the Authority has certainly to apply his mind to the materials before him; but the opinion he forms is a purely subjective matter which depends entirely upon his state of mind. It is of course necessary that he must act in good faith, and if it is established that he was not influenced by any extraneous consideration, there is nothing further to be said about, it. In a judicial proceeding, on the other hand, the process involves the application of a body or rules or principles by the techniques of a particular psychological method It involves a proposals and an opposition, and arriving at a decision upon the same on consideration of facts and circumstances according to the rules of reason and justice It is not necessary that the strict rules of evidence should be followed: the procedure for investigation of facts or for the reception of evidence may vary according to the requirements of a particular case. There need not be any hard and fast rule on such matter, but the decision which the Authority arrives at must not be his 'subjective', 'personal' or 'private' opinion. It must be something which conforms to an objective standard or criteria laid down or recognised by law, and the soundness or otherwise of the determination must be capable of being tested by the same external standard." (p.239-40).

Further in the same judgment, Mukherjee J., observed : "Leaving aside the cases, where the existence of a duty to act judicially is sought to be inferred from the provisions of a statute relating to holding of inquiry or hearing of objections, the general rule that all the cases laid down is that if the foundation of the exercise of the powers by an Authority in his personal satisfaction or subjective opinion about certain facts, the function is to be regarded as executive and not judicial. The facts may undoubtedly be and often are objective facts about which the Authority has to form his opinion. When a statute says that a Minister can requisition property or order compulsory purchase if he deems it expedient to do so in the interest of public safety or the defence of the real, the condition precedent is not the actual existence of the national interest but his own opinion or belief that exists. To quote the words of Lord Radeliffe : 'If the question whether the condition has been satisfied is to be conclusively decided by the man who wields the power the value of the intended restraint is in fact nothing. [32]

"On the other hand if the statute imposes an objective condition precedent of fact to the exercise of powers by an Authority, and not merely his subjective opinion about, the function would be prima facie judicial. The distinction is beautifully illustrated by Lord Atkin in his classic judgment in Liversidge's case. If it is a condition to the exercise of powers by A that X has a right of way or Y, has a broken ankle, the Authority is charged with determining these facts and it must ascertain judicially whether the conditions are fulfilled or not. If, on the other and, the condition is that the Authority thinks or is of

---

32. Nakkudda Ali V. Jayratne at p.242

opinion that X has a right of way or y has a broken ankle, the condition is a purely subjective condition and the act cannot be a judically act, as the existence of the condition is incapable of being determined by a third party by application of any rule of law or procedure.[33]

According to this view if the determination of certain questions is to be arrived at by a subjective process, the act is administrative but, if the question is to be approached objectively it is of judicial character. On the other hand, the majority view is that even if the matter is to be decided subjectively, it would not necessarily imply that the Authority deciding the matter was under a duty to act judicially. The duty to act judicially will only be held to be imposed if the statute imposing the duty to decide requires that incoming to the decision, leading to the administrative action, well recognised principles of judicial approach should be followed. In other words, the duty must be to act as if the Authority was a court or a judge though not necessarily bound to follow the entire collaborate procedure of a law court. The essentials of a judicial procedure need only to be prescribed. These consist in giving an opportunity to the party which is to be affected by an order to make a representation, making some kind of inquiry, hearing and weighing evidence, if any, and considering all the facts and circumstances bearing on the merits of a controversy that appear in decision affecting the rights of one or more parties. In many subsequent decision.[34] Supreme Court followed the authority of Khushal Das Advani V. Province of Bombay[35]. In 1965, Supreme Court in A.C. Companies V. P.N. Sharma"[36] and Shri Bhagwan V. Ramchand[37] approved Ridge V. Baldwin"[38] and observed : "In other words according to

---

33. Ibid.,
34. Nagendra Nath V. Commissioner of Hill Division, A.I.R. (1958) S.C. 398; Radhey Shyam V. State of M.P., A.I.R. (1959) S.C. 107; Nageshwara Rao V. A.P.S.R.T. Corporation,(1959) S.C. 308; Shivaji V. Union of India. A.I.R. (1960) S.C. 196; Board of High School V. Ghanshyam. A.I.R. (1962) S.C. 1110.
35. A.I.R. (1954 S.C. 222.
36. A.I.R. (1965), S.C. 1595.
37. A.I.R. (1965), S.C. 1768

Lord Reid's judgement, the necessity to follow, judicial procedure and principles of natural justice, flow from nature of decision It would thus seen that the area where the principles of natural justice have to be followed and judicial approach has to be adopted, has become wider and consequently, the horizon of writ jurisdiction has been extended in corresponding measure. In dealing with the question as to whether any impinged orders could be revised order Art. 226 of our Constitution, the test prescribed by Lord Reid in this judgement may afford considerable assistance".[39]

However, a change in Law has again been noticed in 1970 where in A.K. Kraipeak V. Union of India[40] the Supreme Court of India approving Lord Parkar's observation in In rett. K. (an infant)"[41] emphasised on the Justness of the decision. Their Lordships also laid down that if an administrative action effects the rights of subjects then principles of natural justice must be followed. The Supreme Court observed:

"The dividing line between an administrative power and quasi-judicial power is quite thin and is being gradually obliterated. .... In a Welfare State like ours which is regulated and controlled by the rule of law, it is inevitable that the jurisdiction of the administrative bodies is increasing at a rapid rate. The concept of rule of law would lose its validity if the instrumentalities of the State are not charged with duty of discharging their functions in fair and just manner. The requirement of acting judicially in essence is nothing but requirement to act justly and fairly and not arbitrarily".[42]

Thus according to latest cases like State of Orissa V. Doctor Birapani Dei;[43] Suresh Koshy V. University of Kerala[44]: A.K. Kraipeak V. Union of India,[45] L.N. Mathur V. Chancellor,

---

38. (1964), A.C. 40.
39. A.I.R. (1965), S.C. 1595.
40. A.I.R. (1970) S.C. 1150.
41. (1967) 2 Q.B. 617.
42. 42. Ibid.
43. A.I.R. (1967) S.C. 1269.
44. A.I.R. (1969) S.C. 138.

Lucknow University;[46] State of U.P. V. Renusgar Power Com.,[47] etc. there is a tendency of judiciary to emphasis on a fair procedure in every type of act whether administrative or quasi-judicial provided it affects the rights of citizens. Thus in every case every decisions has to be just and fair and a decision may be just and fair if it is arrived at by following a judicial procedure and in such cases there is always a duty to act judicially on the part of the decision maker and he is subject to writ of certiorari. The scope of writ of certiorari has thus become wider in present time. However, the nature of writ jurisdiction being a supervisory jurisdiction over inferior courts, tribunals or principle, threrefore, a writ of certiorari can not be issued to co-ordinate courts. Thus, a high court can not issue a writ of certiorari to another higher court nor can one Bench of a High Court issue a writ to a different Bench of the same High Court.

Though, the judgements/orders of High Court are liable to be corrected under Article 136 of the Constituiton, The high courts are not constituted as inferior courts in our constitutional scheme. Therefore, even the Supreme Court would not issue a writ under Article 32 to a High Court. Further, neither a similar Bench nor a larger Bench of the Supreme Court can issue a writ including a writ of certiorari under Article 32 of the Constitution to any other Bench of the Supreme Court. It is pointed out that Article 32 can be imvoked only for the purpose of enforcement of the Fundamental Rights, confirmed in Part III and it is a settled position in law that no judicial ordered passed by any superior court in judicial proceedings can be said to violate any of the Fundamental Rights enshrined in Part III of Constitutiion.[48]

---

45. A.I.R. (1986) 150.
46. A.I.R. (1986) Allahabad 273.

4 GROUNDS ON WHICH CERTIORARI WILL LIE

(A) GROUNDS

A judicial or quasi-judicial decision of an administrative agency, may be quashed by certiorari on following grounds namely, Excess of Power or Defects of Jurisdiction, Violation of pules of Natural Justice, Abuse of Discretionary Power, Error of Law and Fraud.

The above grounds are considered in detail below.

Introductory: It is settled that a decision of an administrative agency may be reviewed where they have exceeded their jurisdiction and dealt with the matters. They have no power to deal with, and if it is found that the tribunal or an agency went outside its jurisdiction the decision will be quashed. Professor B.Schwartz 'n his Law and Executive has remarked that British law of judicial-view of Executive action has been largely developed as a branch 3f the law of ultra vires. He points out that in British law "review is still focused almost entirely upon the question of vires - the courts it power being limited to checking excess of jurisdiction on the part of the Executive:[49] The nomenclature is here confused. Suppose Magistrate's court (a) tried a case that must be tried on indictment, (b) tried a case that can be tried summarily, but imposed a sentence in excess of legal authority, (c) tried a case that can be tried summarily, imposed a proper sentences but one justice had a pecuriary interest in the result or the proceedings cases (a) and (b) can be called an

---

49. The possible sub-divisions of defect of jurisdiction are: (i) Want or lack of jurisdiction, (ii) excess of jurisdiction and ouster of jurisdiction. S.N. Shukla "Grounds for Certiorari" (1960) S.C.J. 247 at p. 250.

excess of jurisdiction. Case (c) can be said to be within the jurisdiction but contrary to natural justice and liable to be set aside. Since in (e) a court so constituted ought not to have heard the case, it may also be called in excess of jurisdiction, i.e., that court as opposed to that type of court) had no jurisdiction. Thus. there are many things, which come within the purview of 'excess of jurisdiction' although at first sight they might not involve any excess of jurisdiction n the literal sense of the term. The following are the cases of excess of jurisdiction where the decision is liable to be quashed.

(B) EXCESS OF POWER OR DEFECTS OF JURISDICTION

Certiorari is the appropriate remedy to raise the question of jurisdiction. Questions may and do arise where such quasi-judicial body attempts to usurp jurisdiction, which it does not possess. The object of writ of certiorari is to keep the exercise of powers by these quasi-judicial tribunals within the limits of their jurisdiction and not act in excess of their powers.[50] Thus the public authorities, tribunals or officials acting judicially must act intra-vires i.e. within their jurisdiction. They can only do what the law permits them to do and They can not do what the law forbids them to do. If such authority acts beyond its jurisdiction, the courts will issue certiorari to quash its action. Hence it is a basic principle of administrative law that no body can act beyond its powers i.e. no administrative authority can exceed the powers given to it and any action taken by it in excess of is powers is invalid. Therefore, certiorari will issue to correct errors jurisdiction as when the inferior court or tribunal acts without irisdiction[51]" or in excess of it[52]" or fails to exercise its,[53] In other words ...Arisdictional error may arise:

1) **When a body is not properly constituted:** If the body taking decision is not constituted according to law then it has no jurisdiction to take a decision and decision taken by it will

---

50. Bharat Bank Ltd. V. Its Employees, A.I.R. (1950) S.C.p.188
51. Harish Chandra V. Triloki Singh A.I.R. (1955) Allahabad, p. 74.
52. Dhranglibra Chemical Works Ltd. V. Saurashtra State A.I.R. (1955) Sau; p. 33.
53. Kalahasti V. Commissioner of Police A.I.R. (1954) Madras, p.736.

be ultra-vires liable to be quashed by certiorari. For example, in United Commercial Bank V. Workmen"[54] the Industrial Dispute Act provides that the Industrial Tribunal shall consist of three members it was held to be acting without jurisdiction when the tribunal was composed of two members. Similarly, in Ram Bharoshey V. Har Swarup"[55] disciplinary committee of the Bar Council is to consist of three members as per the provisions of the Advocates Act but only two members were present when decision was taken, the court held that body was not properly constituted therefore was not competent to take the decision. However, in Saradara Singh V. State of Punjab"[56] where a committee as per rules constituted consisting of Deputy Commissioner as Chairman and District Revenue Officer, District Sainik Welfare Officer and District Social Welfare Officer as members for the selection of Patwaris, the court held constitution of the body as valid and proper when District Revenue Officer was transferred and his successor had participated in the selection. The court observed that the District Revenue Officer was nominated in his official capacity and therefore by virtue of his office the incumbent in office was entitled to participate in the selection of the candidate.

2) **When the body act in excess of its authority :** Sometimes the body though properly constituted may act beyond its authority. In such cases its action will be invalid being without jurisdiction. For example, if an authority empowered to grant a stage carriage permit for a maximum period of three years but grants the same for five years, the action is clearly beyond jurisdiction. By a notification the Government exempted the mining industry from the purview of the Act, the Assistant Commissioner of Labour lacked jurisdiction to entertain a complaint regarding the dismissal of an employee

---

54. 5 A.I.R.(1951)S.C.p.230,See also Ammal V. Rana A,I.R.(1953) Madras. p 129
55. A.I.R. (1976) S.C. p. 1739.
56. A.I,R. (1991) S.C. p. 2248.

of the Ballarpur Collieries Company which was a part of the mining industry, the court held the action invalid

i. and quashed the same by issuing certiorari.[57] Similarly. where an industrial tribunal entertained a dispute which was not industrial, it was held to have acted in excess of its jurisdiction.[58] The case of Budh Prakash Jai Prakash V. Sales Tax Officer, Kanpur"[59] " is an extreme case. In this case Allahabad High Court quashed by certiorari an order of the Sales Tax Officer under the U.P. Sales Tax Act. The officer levied sales tax on forward contract, irrespective of the place where the delivery took place under the contract. The Allahabad High Court held this to be ulra-vires because the subject matter of levy was outside the scope of the power under the Act. A similar case is Sakhigopal Coconut Growers Co-operative Society V. State of Orissa.[60]

ii. **When the body declines jurisdiction:** A tribunal is said to refuse or decline jurisdiction when it either acts on the direction of some other authority or delegates its jurisdiction to some other authority. In Rajgopalan Naidu V. State Transport Appellate Tribunal"[61] where the Government of Madras issued direction laying down the principles for the issue of stage carriage permits under the Motor vehicles Act by the Regional Transport Authority, the Supreme Court held no directions could be issued to these bodies (quasi-judicial) in the discharge of their quasi-judicial functions because it was against the fundamental principle of the judicial process. A quasi-judicial body cannot be asked to exercise its direction in accordance with the instructions given by some other non-judicial body where a quasi-judicial body acts

---

57. Ballarpur Collieries V. Industrial Court, A.I.R. (1966) S.C. p.925.. 12.
58. Express News paper Ltd. V. Industrial Tribunal A.I.R. (1957) S.C. p. 532
59. A.I.R. (1952) And, p. 764.
60. A.I.R. (1953) Orissa, p. 334.
61. AIR 1964 S.C. 1573

according to such directions, it in effect declines jurisdiction. Similarly in **Bishwanath Nag V. State of Bihar1**[62], the State Government issued a direction to the Regional Transport Authorities under Section 43-A of the Motor Vehicles Act that a family consisting of husband, wife and their minor children will not be allowed more than one stage carriage permit. The East Bihar R.T.A. refused a permit to the petitioner on the basis of the direction of the State Government. The court quashed the order of the tribunal on the ground that the power to issue permit exercised by the authority was a quasi-judicial power and the State Government had no power to ssue directions to control the discretion of the authority.

In **Mahadayal Premchandra V. Commercial Tax Officer"**[63] the Asstt. Commissioner had delegated his power of assessment to the commercial tax officer. When the appellant's assessment came before the latter, he, instead of exercising his own judgement-eferred the same to the former for opinion and decided it in accordance with this opinion. The Supreme Court quashed the action on the ground that the commercial Tax Officer did not exercise the power himself which was an instance of refusal to exercise jurisdiction.

Thus, the most straightforward case for review of all administrative acts is where the tribunal exercised a power not given it by the statute on which it relies. Hence, a decision of an Jthority can be quashed by certiorari if it is taken without jurisdiction has also been observe by the Supreme Court in riEbrahim V.

Custodian General"[64] "Indeed, it must be shown before such a writ (certiorari) is issued that the authority which passed the order acted without jurisdiction or excess of it". In Hari Vishnu Kamath V. Syed Ahamed Ishaque,[65] the Supreme Court

---

62. A AIR 1986 Pat. 59.
63. A.I.R. (1958) S.C. p. 667..
64. A.I.R. (1958) S.C. p. 319.
65. A.I.R.. (1955) S.C. 233, See also State of Punjab V. H.K. Sharma A.I.R. 1966) S.C. Raja Anand Brahma Bhat V. State of U.P., AIR 1967 S.C.

laid down that certiorari will also be issued when the courts or tribunals act without jurisdiction or inexcess of it or fail to exercise it. Recently the Supreme Court quashed even order of a Division Bench of High Court directing the Howrah Municipal Corporation to grant permission 'o the petioner for construction of additional floors above four floors ceing in violation of the amended Building Rules and the resolution of the corporation saying that the said Bench Committed an error in directing grant of sanction to the respondent Company in clear violation of the existing Building Rules and the resolution of the corporation.[66]

(C) VIOLATION OF RULES OF NATURAL JUSTICE

Introduction : Natural Justice is the name given to certain fundamental principles which are so important for the proper exercise of power that they are projected from judicial to administrative sphere. In English Law Natural Justice performs a function similar to that of procedural due process as it exists in America.

In the field of administrative law the concept of natural justice, as observed by the United States Supreme Court, means 'Fundamentals of fair play'. The Committee on Ministers Powers explain the conception as follow

"(The) Phrase (Natural Justice) is perhaps more often used than understood, and we therefore, venture to say what we understand by it. Before doing so, however, it may be well to call attention to two cases - Bachanan V. Rucket[67] and Schibaby V. N. VVestenblz"[68] which show that the conception of 'Natural Justice' must be regarded as belonging to the field of moral and social principles and not as having passed into the category of substantive law, so as necessarily to make every act obnoxious to its canons a transgression of a legal rule recognised and enforced

---

1081 and Marathwad University V. S.B.R. Chavan A.I.R. (1989) S.C. 1582. where the Supreme Court quashed by issuing certiorari the decisions taken in excess authority.
66. Hawrah Municipal Corporation V. Gangas Rope Co. Ltd. (2004) ISCC 663.
67. 19 (1807) 1 Camp. p. 66.
68. (1870) L.R.6 Q.B. p. 155.

by our courts But although 'Natural Justice' does not fall within those definite and well recognised rules of law which English courts of law enforce, we think it is beyond doubt that there are certain canons of judicial conduct to which all tribunals and persons who have to give judicial or quasi-judicial decisions ought to conform. The principles on which they rest are we think implicit in the rule of law".

Acceptance of the principles of natural justice throughout the common law world, as a cordial requirement of administrative adjudicatory procedure, has gone a long way to relieve the agony of the individual in getting justice at the hands of bureaucracy. He is now assured of a minimum deal of fairness which if denied to him, will render the administrative adjudication liable to be struck down by the higher courts. It is now beyond doubt that all tribunals and administrative authorities while exercising quasi-judicial or even administrative powers are under an obligation to conform to the above canons of judicial conduct. Thus, Lord Hewart's dictum that :

"Justice should not only be done but should manifestly and undoubtedly be seen to be done[69] is realised to a great extent in its application to administrative adjudication.

The purpose of the rules is clear enough - it is simply to ensure that there shall be a fair hearing. The conception of natural justice certainly observes two propositions. First, no party ought to be condemned unheard; Second. a man must not be judge in his own cause. These two propositions are discussed below: In Kanda V. Malaya,[70] Lord Denning observed:

"The rule against bias is one thing. The right to be heard another. These two rules are essential. characteristics of what is often called natural justice. They are twin pillars supporting it. The Romans put them in the maxims: Nemo Judex in Causa Sua; and Audi Alteram partem. They have recently been put in two words, impartiality and fairness. But they are separate concepts and are governed by separate considerations".

---

69. Rex V. Susex Justices (1924) 1 K.B.
70. (1962) A.C. 322

The conditions of application of rules of natural justice are changing from time to time and at present the emphasis is on fairness and justness of the decision and the rules of N.J. are applicable to judicial, quasi-judicial as well as administrative decisions as the aim of the rules is to secure justice or to prevent miscarriage of justice. Now the requirement of acting judicially in essence is nothing but a requirement to act justly and fairly and not arbitrarily.[71] Thus the present position is that the rules of natural justice are to be applied whether the act of the administration is judicial, quasi-judicial or administrative for a fair and just decision i.e. the principles of natural justice apply to the exercise of the administrative powers as well.[72]

The concept of natural justice represents in itself certain basic and eternal values that have been cherished by the human civilization since creation. These basic values find their fine expression in the Ancient Indian concept of Rabibh-Nyaya, Dharma-Nyaya or Yokti Nyaya. This concept of justice is the general principle of law common to all civilized communities. They belong to the common consciousness of the mankind. This concept is ultimate values that are the matter of belief and conviction. They are proof in themselves and carry with them their own evidence of existence. They are the unwritten codes no doubt, yet their violations put the violators in disgrace.

The rules of natural justice are the rules of process values. They guarantee that decisions have been taken in a just, reasonable and fair manner. They concern themselves with the procedures. Even if the decisions result in the deprivation of certain rights of the litigants, by insisting upon the fair procedures, the rules engender among the litigants the satisfaction that injustice has not been done to them, and the decisions have been pronounced after affording them an opportunity to rebut the charges made against them by an

---

71. A.K. Kraipeak V. Union of India, A.I.R. (1970) S.C. 150.
72. 24 Per Hegde J. in C.B. Boarding and Lodging, Bangalore V. State of Mysore A.I.R. (1970) S.C. 2042 at 2050. See also Him Singh V. Union of India (1970) Lab. I.C. 593 (Delhi).

impartial adjudicatory body in a detached manner, that the decisions are accompanied by reasons and have been given in a just, reasonable and fair manner and in good faith. They are the fountains of justice from where all laws, rules and regulations have come. It ensures that not only this fountain remains pure but the streams from it also flow in a pure and satisfying way. The aim of natural justice is to secure justice or to prevent miscarriage of justice. However, while our judiciary has been insisting upon the adherence to the rules of natural justice in every decisional process that affects the rights, liberty, reputation, livelihood and other civil consequence, the practical aspect of the decisional process sometimes shocks the very conscience of the men.

FIRST PRINCIPLE OF NATURAL JUSTICE

The principle of natural justice are well settled.[73] The first and foremost principle is one which has two aspects. No party ought to be condemned unheard and if his right to be heard is to be a reality he must know in good time the case which he has to meet. This principle is enshrined in the maxim "Audi alteram oartem". As put by justice Barle in an American case.[74]

"It is a rule founded upon the first principle of natural justice, older than written constitutions, that a citizen shall not be deprived of life, liberty or property without an opportunity to be heard in defence of his rights; and the constitutional provision that no person shall be deprived of his rights of these 'without due process of law' has its foundation in this rule."[75]

Historical development of the rule

Most of the earliest decisions in which the rule was applied concerned summary proceedings before justices. In Buchaman V. Rucker (1817), Lord Pllenbouough declared at nisi prius that it was contrary to the first principles of reason and justice that either in civil or criminal proceedings a man should

---

73. Burhanuddin Hussain V. State of Andhra Pradesh, A.I.R. (1970) A.P. 137.
74. 74 N.Y. 183.
75. Ibid. at p. 190.

be condemned before he was heard and that, "the practice of the Law Courts of Tobago to summon a defendant who was out of the jurisdiction and never had been within it by railing the writ on the door of the court-housewas male praxis (had practicer. In other words the rule was first applied to acts which were purely judicial, such as the acts of magistrates administering criminal law. Next the rule was extended to the acts of bodies of more ambiguous status such as the court of the Vice-Chancellor at Cambridge which in 1718 deprived Dr. Bently of his degrees. In the well known case of Capel V. Child[76], where a bishop, empowered by statute to order a vicar to appoint a curats when satisfied, either of his own knowledge or by affidavit, that the vicar had neglected his duties, was held to be under a duty to give the vicar notice and opportunity to be heard before making the order. Then there was a further extension, where a statute authorizing to interfere with property or rights was silent on the question of notice and hearing, the courts, drawing upon the authority of old cases, invoked, 'the justice of the common law' to supply the omission of the legislature'. Next, the rule was applied to the organs of local government, such as Vestries; Boards of Health and Boards of works, "The powers exercised by these bodies were plainly administrative; but nevertheless, the courts called them judicial, so that they could apply to them the principle that powers of any kind must not be exercised without due inquiry into facts.

   The courts in England thus made considerable progress towards establishing a general code of administrative procedure cy developing the doctrine of audi alteram partem. The law reports contain striking examples of purely executive action, taken within The express authority of an Act of Parliament, which were nevertheless been held illegal because the person affected was not heard. Of these cases, it sufficient to refer to Cooper V. Wordsworth Board of VVorks"[77] and Hopkins V. Smithwick Board of Health.[78] In the Cooper case, the Board of works were

---

76. 149 Eng. Rap. 235.
77. (1863) 14 C.B. (N.S.) 180.

empowered by statute to pull down a house where the builder had neglected to give notice of his intention to build seven days before proceeding to dig or lay the foundation. The court held that the function was judicial to the extent that the principles of natural justice applied and that, accordingly, the Board of Works had to give the builder an opportunity of defending himself before pulling down the house. In the Hopkins case the local Board of health had statutory power to pull down buildings erected in contravention of local by laws. The builder had knowingly erected a building in contravention of such local by laws. The court of Appeal held that the Board of Health must give the builder an opportunity of being heard before pulling down his building.

As the case law developed, audi atleram partem acquired various refinements and also certain limits. The turning point of the case law was the notable decisions of the House of Lords in Local Government Board V. Arlidge,[79] where it was held that an objector was not entitled, on grounds of natural justice, to know which official of the Board actually decided the case, or to see the report made by the Board Inspector after the public inquiry. It was at this point that the court called a halt to the application of judicial technique to administrative decisions.

A failure to give a proper hearing may quite properly be regarded as one of the grounds for the issue of writ of certiorari : In Mineral Development Ltd. V. State of Bihar[80] the order of the State of Bihar dated 7.9.1955, canceling the petitioners license was quashed and mandamus issued directing the respondent to forbear from giving effect to the said order of cancellation of license on the grounds, among others of canceling the lease without affording the petitioners reasonable opportunity to show cause. Many leading cases, both ancient and modern, can be cited where it has been held that if a person has not first been fairly heard"[81] in his own defence the power has not been exercised

---

78. (1990) 24 Q.B.D. 712.
79. (1915) A.C. 13
80. 32 (A.I.R.) (1960) S.C. 468.

fairly, both in appearance and reality. As to the judicial review of administrative acts the courts in India hold that it is not easy to find in the words of the statute the principle of audi alteram partem or the rules of natural justice, The rules of natural justice have to be importedin a proceeding even when the statute is silent.[82]

This principle of natural justice has many facets, for example right to cross examination, representation by lawyer. post iecisional hearing etc.

Right to cross-examination : Refusal to permit cross-examination of writ at an administrative hearing will usually be a denial of natural justice.[83] After the decision of Supreme Court Verma's case."[84] It must be taken as settled principle that ordinarily ,vhere the evidence of witnesses is relied on as against a party in a quasi-judicial proceedings, natural justice requires that the party affected should have the opportunity to cross-examination such .witnesses, because a person cannot be said to have an adequate opportunity unless he has an opportunity of destroying that case by cross-examination. The right to cross-examination is not absolute right. There are instances where the violation of this rule of natural justice has resulted in meeting out the essence of justice. In Hari Nath V. Rajendra Medical College, Ranchi" [85] the appellants were male student of the respondent college who had been expelled from the college by the principal on the charge of `nude march in a girls hostel. The Inquiry Committee report was not made available to the students. No opportunity was given to cross-examine the witnesses and inquiry was held behind the back of the appellants. The Supreme Court did not read any violation of the principles of natured

---

81. For example see Principal Medical College. Pondicherry V. M.J. Vincent.
82. 34 M.A.Fazal, Judicial control of Administrative Action in India and Pakistan See also Shri Bhagwan V. Ram Chand A.I.R. (1965) S.C. 1767.
83. 35 R.V,Edmanton J.J. exp.Brooks(1960)1W.L.R. 697, Blaise V. Blaise (1969)p. 54.
84. 36 (1968) S.C.R. 499, p. 507
85. A.I.R. (1973) S.C. 1260.

Sustice because the girls, who were affected, would not have otherwise come forward to give evidence for fear of retaliation and harassment. The students were given an opportunity to state their case. Nothing more was to be done on the facts and circumstances of the case. In K.L. Tripathi V. State Bank of India,[86] the court observed that "In order to sustain a complaint of violation of principles of natural justice on the ground of absence of opportunity of cross-examination, it has to be established that procedure followed. Neither the cross examination nor the opportunity to lead the evidence by the delinquent is an integral part of all quasi-judicial adjudication". Cross-examination is no doubt one of the most efficacious methods of establishing truth and exposing falsehood. in Ram Narayan Keshori V. University of Calcutta,[87] the court insisted that natural justice should not be illusory, futile or an empty formality. Opportunity of cross-examination is an important aspect of ;air hearing and it should not be denied, but there are circumstances Nhere the right to cross-examination may not produce the desired -esult. Hence exceptions are permitted to this right.

It must be made clear here that technical rules of evidence io not apply to quasi-judicial tribunals. Technical rules of evidence 'form no part of the rules of natural justice, that "the personis charging quasi-judicial functions can take into account any matter which has probative value, the weight to be attached to the evidence being a matter for such person"[88]. The procedure to be generally followed is that the party interested in taking action should examine its witnesses first, allow them to be cross-examined and then ask the charged person to give his explanation and to -ebut the evidence laid against him.

Representation by Lawyer

Representation by a lawyer in the hearing procedure has been nigh lighted by the judiciary by holding that denial to egal

---

86. 38 A.I.R. (1984) S.C. 273.
87. A.I.R. (1982) Cal, 1.
88. Seervai, op. cit. 1452.

representation in itself amounts to denial of reasonable opportunity of hearing. As a general rule any party before a tribunal be represented by a lawyer or it is covered by the principle of natural justice, it can not be said assertively. In practice the position is that the representation is freely permitted except in rare cases where it is restricted by regulation.

In earlier period there were certain restrictions on representation by qualified lawyers, but they were removed in 1958 by the Tribunal And Inquiries Act. Prof. Wade says: "The right to representation by a lawyer or other person may prove to be a part of N.J. in suitable cases, but this is not as yet clearly established. It probably exists in the case of a formal tribunal or investigation if there is no provision to the contrary, but regulations excluding it have been upheld. In cases concerning non-statutory domestic tribunals the Court of Appeal has favoured the right of legal representation where a serious charge was made, but has held that it may be excluded by an association's rules.[89] It is also excluded, as same Court has held, in disciplinary proceedings, which demand a rapid hearing and decision, as in the case of offenses committed by orisoners. Nor can it apply where an oral hearing need not be given at all.[90] It is clear, therefore, that one who is entitled to appear in oerson before statutory tribunal is also entitled, in the absence of express or implied provision to the contrary,"[91] to be represented oy a lawyer or by any other appropriate spokeman of his choice except in informal proceedings before a domestic tribunal.[92] Prof. de Smith says that "it would be contrary to natural justice to allow one side to be legally represented but to refuse the same right to the other. One must recall that natural justice demand only minimum standard of fair adjudication and not ideal standards. The reasons for excluding legal representations are

---

89. Enderly town Football Club Ltd.V. Football Association Ltd.(1971) Ch. 591.
90. Wade, Op. Cit. 485. 43 Maynard V. Osmand (1977) Q.B. 240.
91. Maynard V. Osmand (1977) Q.B. 240.
92. Enderly Town Football Club Ltd.V .Football Association Ltd. (1971) C.H 591.

various: they tend to introduce too much formality. they disturb witnesses, their presence increases the likelihood of subsequent proceedings in the courts. In general, legal representation of the right quality before statutory tribunal is desirable, and that a person threatened with social or financial ruin by disciplinary proceedings in a :purely domestic forum may be gravely prejudiced if he is denial legal representation. Development of the case-law on implied rights to legal representation in non-statutory environments should be guided by a realistic apraisal of the interests of the person claiming it, as well as of the interests of the organisation to which he belongs".[93]

Seervai argues that on the question of principality is submitted that unless there consideration of public policy overriding the claims of natural justice in any particular class of matters, the assistance of counsel or agent is necessary if a person is to have a fair opportunity to meet the case against him".[94]

J.E. Alder summarises the position with regard to legal representation in the following words :

1. In the context of a statutory and domestic tribunal a prima facie right to representation exist upon the basis of agency. Such a right includes the freedom to select a lawyer.
2. This right can be excluded by contract in which a provision will be contained to this effect.
3. Unless the selected representative is 'manifestly in proper'. the tribunal can not exclude the right of representation in its discretion.
4. The statutory body must expressly refer to the question of representation in the statute.[95]

In Jackson V. Napper. Reschmidit's Trade Mark"[96] Stirling, J. outlined the law relating to representation by agent. He said "but prima facie, when there is nothing said about it, a person has

---

93. deSmith, op.cit. p. 213, 214.
94. Seenai, op. cit. 1451.
95. Representation before tribunal (1972) Public Law 278.
96. (1887) 35 C.H.D. 162 at p. 172.

the same right of appointing an agent for the purpose of exercising a statutory right as for only other purpose." In ***R. V. Many Abbotts Association Committee"*[97] a mandamus was granted to compel the committee to hear the objection by an agent who was neither a member of the legal profession nor the member of the aggrieved person family. In the courts opinion the committee was under the duty to hear and determine objection, they could not refuse to hear the objector's representatives.

Apparently, therefore, at common law where a person may appear personally, he may depute an agent to represent him. It means that exclusion of the right to a personal hearing also excludes the representation by an agent.

Lord 'Denning' insisted in Pet V. Greyhound Racing Association Ltd.[98] that "The charge concerns his reputation and livelihood, and on such an inquiry he is entitled not only to appear by himself but also to appoint an agent to act for him. Even a prisoner can have his friend." Davis L.J. agreed with Master of rolls and said that in circumstances which might mean a great deal to a person who was licensed by a club as to his future and livelihood he should be entitled to have legal representation unless express words in the rules deny him such a right. Russel, L.J. also said the same.

This case is of particular interest to member of academic profession because it raises question whether an University or School must give a student an opportunity to be represented by council, whenever serious question of discipline arises. "It is probable that 50 years ago the court would have held that they were not required to do so, but it is likely that today they would reach an opposite conclusion" [99]

However. Lord Denning in Enderly Town Football Club's case" [100] said that much depended on the Club's rule. where they were silent there was no absolute right to legal representation as

---

97. (1891) 1 Q.B. 378.
98. (1968) 2 W.L.R. 1471.
99. Wade, 'Natural Justice and Disciplinary Inquiries' 84, L.C.R.451.
100. (1971) C.H. 591.

it was within the tribunal discretion and in many cases it would be a good thing for the proceeding of a domestic tribunal to be conducted informally without legal representation. If the point of law did arise, it was open for the parties to seek the courts guidance. He, however, warned that tribunal could not fetter its discretion as rules of policy must be directory and not imperative.

C.P. 'Seepersad'[101] is of the view that legal representation before administrative tribunal is not a pre-requisite of the audi alteram partem rule. Where however, the tribunal consists of the legally qualified personnel, or one party to the issue is represented legally, then it is sensible to grant the other party the same privilege. In cases where a large fine is to be imposed or a man may be deprived of his livelihood or property or his office, justice demands that he be allowed legal representation. Denial in These cases would possibly be void. The universal introduction of lawyers in the tribunal system would evoke delay and expenses and detract from the informality of the administrative tribunal. The Franks Committee recommended that right to legal -epresentation should be curtailed only in the most exceptional circumstances. In the U.S.A. the right to legal representation is guaranteed for many purposes, by the combined effect of the 'due process' clause of the American Constitution and Section (6) of the American Administrative Procedure Act.

There are two views about the role of lawyers in administrative proceeding. The first view is the traditional one. t favours the right to legal representation in all cases. Many parties before administrative tribunal are incapable of their own of adequately preparing or presenting their case. The issues are too complicated, technical, the party does not understood the nature or forms of proceeding, the party lacks the necessary intelligent and is too nervous to do justice to him own cause. This view has found wide spread.

---

101. Public Law(1975) p. 248. Fairness and Audi Alteram.

The other view is that absence of lawyers in dministrative proceedings is good things. The introduction of awyers leads to greater formality, unnecessary argument over technicalities, longer hearing and increased cost, thus largely efeating advantages of the proceedings. Lawyers do not know the matter of specialised and technical character which many tribunals deal with. Consequently, there is need for specialist advocate nstead of or in addition to ordinary practicing lawyers.

Willheim"[102] is of the view that exclusion of legal representation is not wide spread in the commonwealth world. Thisprinciple is based on substantial ground that lawyers can not remain in different to the important development of economic and social affairs that lie behind this trend. Rather they should seek to ive guidance and leadership in the creation of new legal concepts, institutions and techniques. However, participation may take various forms. *Harry Whit* More,[103] concludes that the situation in the United Kingdom is far from being satisfactory. The fact is that the Franks Committee's idea of an informal atmosphere in which an ordinary man may have a fair hearing is just not working. It seems that legal representation, or indeed any representation is, no exception, rather than the rule. All tribunal flow from the lack of adequate legal assistance and representation. The commonest situation before tribunal is that the claimant or party is completely inarticulate. Sometimes he is literally trembling before the tribunal or merely mumbles a few words. In many cases the applicant is confrontal by an official or an employer or land lord's solicitor who has the fact fully marshaled and is prepared to argue the point at issue.

He suggests that the quality of legal representation must be stressed. There is 'the party mason' in real life - the criminal lawyer for excellence. He can do an immense amount of harm. The lawyer will insist that prehearing procedure and hearing

---

102. Legal representation before administrative tribunal. E.Will-Heim. The Australian Law Journal, 1969, p. 64.
103. The role of Lawyers in Administrative Jutice.Whit More, Harry, 33M. L.R.

before an administrative body he exactly the same as in the superior courts. Thus it will turn the whole process in an adversely trial. Much technicalities are also emphasized upon. Sometimes a lawyers thinks that administrative adjudication is beneath his dignity. He says that "in its own interest and in the interest of the public the legal profession ought to recognise and obligation to improve the competence of its members who appear before tribunal and administration".

In R. V. Home Secretary, ex. p. Teriant,[104] Webster, J. intensies the consideration that were relevant to the exercise of the discretion of Board and quashed the decision of Board as the Board has never considered exercising its discretion to permit legal representation. In addition, in the muting charge, the court ruled, it should be unreasonable for any Board to refuse legal representation in view of the gravity and complexity of the charge. He held that while 'Tarrant' had no "right" to legal representation, he had in favour of granting legal representation.

This judgement harps back to the Pre-Ridge V. Baldwin, when courts stressed that bodies were masters of their own procedures subject only to residual control by the courts, "C. B. Lewis" is of the view that "The courts should once again be abdicating their responsibility for structuring the manner in which decisions are taken. Secondly, the court in this case adopted excessive review without considering whether in less serious assault charges there was a right' to legal representation or not and whether its refusal by the Board was really unreasonable. Legal representation is not a distinct right."[105]

Position under Indian Law

Though, ordinarily courts should discourage the involvement of legal practitioners in domestic inquiries in order to avoid delay and complexity. nonetheless, the court cannot ignore that in exceptional cases a representation by lawyer is necessary, otherwise there may be failure of the inquiry itself and a denial of a proper and effective defence.

---

104. (1984) 1, All. E.R. 799.
105. (1984) Public Law, p. 401.

The need for lawyer representation has been felt more in a domestic inquiry because there the men of the establishment perform the job of the judge. In deciding such cases the nature of inquiry, the atmosphere and other situations are to be taken into account.

The legal position at present is that though legal representation is not an essential element of natural justice in all cases, the claim for legal representation should normally be left to the discretion of the court to be allowed in exceptional cases. In fact, though, the courts will not actively encourage participation by lawyers in domestic inquiries, such circumstances should not be used for unfairness and, therefore, whenever necessary, in the facts of the case, it is for the court to grant or not, permission. This position of law flows from the several decisions of Supreme Court. In Kalindi V. Tata Locomotive and Engineering Co. Ltd."[106] and in Brooke Bond India Ltd. V. Subba Raman"[107] the court held that a workman has no right to be represented at such inquiry by a representative of his union, though, of course, an employee, in his discretion, can and may allow his employee to avail himself of such assistance. In Dunlop Rubber Co. V. their Workmen,[108] the court observed that where the Standing Order allows the workman to be represented by a representative of a recognised union, the aid of representation must be allowed.

In C.L. *Subramanyam* V. Collector of Customs"[109] the court held that delinquent had the right for legal representation. But again in S.C. Sarin V. Union of India"[110] the court held that denial of legal representation, to a deliquent employee, would not vitiate the inquiry.

The court held the same view in Standard Pottery Works V. Standard Pottery Works Employees Union[111]. In fact the

---

106. A.I.R. (1960) S.C., 914.
107. (1961) 2 LAB LJ, 417
108. A.I.R. (1965) S.C.. 1392.
109. A.I.R. (1972) S.C.. 2178
110. A.I.R. (1976) S.C., 1686.
111. (1981) LAB IC, 1132.

practice where it can be allowed and where it has to be refused cannot be ascertained as uniform. In Braja Kishore V. State of Orissa"[112] refusal of legal aid was justified. On the other hand in Nityaranjan V. State[113], Nripendra Nath Baqchi V. Secretary to Government of West Bengal[114], Bhagat Ram V. State of H.P.[115], it has been held that refusal to legal representation would vitiate the inquiry whereas in Krishna Chandra V. Union of India[116]. Ameeteep Machine Tools V. Labour Court, Haryana[117], it was held that legal representation would not help the inquiry proceeding.

Our Supreme Court held in Board of Trustees of the Port of Bombay V. Dilip Kumar[118]" that "In our view we have reached a stage in our onward march to fair play in action that where in an inquiry before a domestic tribunal the delinquent officer is pitted against a legally trained mind, if he seeks permission to appear through a legal practitioner. the refusal to grant this request would amount to denial of reasonable request to defend himself and the essential principles of natural justice would be violated.

The Bombay High Court has observed that if the petitioner is not allowed a legal representation, Article 21 of the Constitution will also be violated as the word 'life' has been given a wider interpretation by the court as including the right to livelihood, and if the outcome of the departmental inquiry is likely to adversely affect reputation or livelihood of a person some of the final graces of human civilization which make the life worth-living would be jeopardised. Justice must not only be done but must seem to be done is not an euhemerism for courts alone it applied with equal vigour and rigour to all those who must be responsible for fair play in action. And a quasi-judicial tribunal cannot view the matter with equaminity or inequality of representation".[119]

---

112. A.I.R. (1965) Orissa, 183.
113. A.I.R. (1962) Orissa. 78.
114. A.I.R. (1961) Calcutta, 1.
115. A.I.R. (1983) S.C., 454.
116. A.I.R. (1974) S.C., 1589.
117. A.I.R.(1980) S.C., 2135.
118. (1983) LAB IC. 419.

The Kerala High Court has held in P.P. Gopalan V. the D.I.G.[120]" that permission of legal representation is the minimal requirement of the rule to enable him to have a proper representation. In Mohan Chandran and Others V. Union of India[121] Madhya Pradesh High Court held that the refusal of assistance of an advocate has in fact resulted in a serious prejudice to the petitioners and also a denial of reasonable opportunity of defending themselves, against the charges leveled against them. However, in C. Ramanathan V. Senior Regional Manager, Pal.. Madras[122], the Madras N.C. had held that if the petitioner failed to name another person for representing him in place of the person nominated, and those to participate in the inquiry proceeding that would not vitiate the inquiry.

Thus, legally speaking; an employee is not entitled to legal representation as a matter of right. However, the employer in his discretion can and may allow his employees to avail himself of such assistance. This word 'may' in appropriate cases means must. However, refusal by the inquiry officer to allow workman to be represented by a person of his choice does not vitiate inquiry.

The broad criterion here is that a representation should be allowed if there is a specific provisions or rule to that effect, or if, in the interests of fair play, such representation is necessary. Mr. Lakshmi Swaminathan suggests that"[123] " under Article 311 (2) of the Indian Constitution reasonable opportunity to be heard should not be given a narrow scope. Legal representation, if he so desires, to the civil servant against whom disciplinary action is taken, should not be denied to him the courts saying that he can by his age, experience, number of witnesses, nature of evidence and charges, effectively conduct his own defence, the court

---

119. Antonio B. Furtede V. Chairman and Managing Director, Bank of India, (1986) LAB IC, Bombay H.C., 613.
120. (1986) LAB IC, Kerala H.C. 980.
121. (1986) LAB IC, 1245, M.P. High Court.
122. 74 (1986) LAB IC, 1504, Madras High Court.
123. A Civil Servant Right to be represented in Disciplinary Proceeding, 16 J.I.L.T. (1974) p. 282.

should in the interpretation of Article 311(2), lean more in favour of legal representation in such cases, than give it a restrictive meaning, because to err on this wider meaning would be less harmful in the circumstances. Besides one must also not forget that a lawyer would be an important, actor in the stage of a 'life and death' drama which a civil servant tries to enact against a powerful colossus viz., the government machinery who has all the brains. power and finances at its disposal. It is necessary to give the civil servant a right to be represented by the Counsel and the law should be suitably amended and made clear on this point.

Post-Decisional Hearing : Post decisional hearing has added a new dimension to the principle of audi alteram partem. The basic foundation of this is that audi alteram partem rule is sufficiently flexible to permit modifications and variations to suit the exigencies of myriad kinds of situations which may arise. The person affected must have a reasonable opportunity of being heard. What opportunity may be regarded as reasonable would necessarily depend on the practical necessities of the situation. "It may be a sophisticated full-fledged hearing or it may be a hearing which is very brief and minimal; it may be a hearing prior to the decision or it may be even post decisional remedial hearing"76[124]

'deSmith' writes that "Recent case-law indicates that the courts are increasingly favouring an approach based in large part upon an assessment of whether, in a particular context, the procedure as a whole gave the individual an opportunity for a fair hearing. Thus, when provision is made by statute or by the rules of a voluntary association for a full re-hearing of the case by the original body or some other body vested with and exercising original jurisdiction, a court may readily conclude that a full and fair rehearing will cure any defect in the original decision".[125]

In Calvin V. Carr, the court refused to lay down an absolute rule with regard to post-decisional hearing. It says, "The conclusion is reached that a complainant has the right to nothing

---

124. Maneka Gandhi V. Union of India (1978) 1 S.C.C, 291.
125. deSmith, op. cit. 245

less than a fair hearing both at the original and at the appeal stage:[126] Maneka Gandhi's decision has expanded the horizons of natural justice. The court has laid down that if in a situation, pre-decisional hearing is not feasible, then post-decisional hearing may be given rather than denying hearing altogether. But post-decisional hearing procedure must be used restrictively and not as a substitute for pre-decisonal hearing as far the person affected, pre-decisional hearing is a much better safeguard. Maneka Gandhi thus achieved universalisation of the hearing procedure in the administrative process. The post-decisional hearing theory has been followed by the court in Mohinder Sing Gill V. Chief Election Commissioner[127] S.L. Kapoor V. Jagmohan[128], Swadeshi Cotton Mills V. Union of India[129], C.J.T. V. B.N.Bhattacharjee"[130] and Liberty Oil Mills V. Union of India[131]. In liberty Oil Mills case the court stated: "Natural justice will be violated if the authority refuses to consider the request of the aggrieved party for an opportunity to make his representation against the export adinterim orders"[132]. The court has reiterated the same in Union of India V. Tulsi Ram Pate1[133]. Satyavir Singh V. Union of India[134]" and Ramchandra V. Union of India[135]. Thus, the post-decisional hearing has brought a new prospect for the evolution of the principle of audi alteram partem It is not something novel to Indian jurisprudence. The Industries (Development and Regulation) Act 1951[136]" and the Income Tax Act 1961[137]" provide for the post decisional hearing. However, for the first time this concept was transplanted into the soil of administrative law in our country by Bhagwati, J. in Maneka

---

126. (1979) 2 W.L.R. 755.
127. 78. (1975) 1 S.C.C, 783, 405.
128. A.I.R. (1973) S.C., 205.
129. A.I.R. (1981) S.C., 818.
130. A.I.R. (1979) S.C., 1725.
131. A.I.R. (1984) S.C., 1271.
132. Ibid. at 1285.
133. AIR 1985 S.C. 1482,
134. AIR 1986 S.C. 556 at 569
135. AIR 1986 S.C. 1171 at 1181.
136. 88 Section 18 A.
137. Section 132 (5).

Gandhi's case. If there is novelty, that novelty is in this respect. It must be remembered that post-decisional hearing is not a substitute for pre-decisional hearing in administrative decision making.

The idea of post-decisional hearing has been developed to maintain to balance between administrative efficiency and fairness to the individual. However, one cannot expect that a post decisional hearing would be anything more than a mere empty formality as has also been observed by the Supreme Court in **Trehan V. Union of India[138]**; "In our opinion, the post-decisional opportunity of hearing does not subserve the rules of natural justice. The authority who embarks upon a post decisional hearing will normally proceed with a closed mind and there is hardly any chance of getting proper consideration of the representation at such post-decisional opportunity".

Exclusion of the Audi Alteram Partem

The audi alteram partem rule is not an absolute rule. It has got some exceptions also. This rule may be excluded by the very nature of the power, for instance where urgent action has to be taken to safeguard public health, by the absence of 'legitimate expectations'; by the dubious doctrine that a hearing would make no difference, by the refusal of remedies in discretion, and by the rule that employees can be dismissed at pleasure.

In truth the lesson of the host of cases that have been brought before the courts is that "exceptions are conspicuous by their absence wherever genuine administrative power has been exercised under statute with any serious effect on a man's property, liberty or livelihood where a right to be fairly heard has been denied, it is more probably a case of a bad decision than of a true exception"[139].

The word 'exception' is really a minomer because in these exclusionary cases, the audi alteram partem rule is held inapplicable not by way of an exception to 'fair-play inaction', but

---

138. (1989) 1 S.C.C. 704.
139. Wade, op. cit, 506.

because nothing unfair can be inferred by not affording an opportunity to present or meet a case"[140]

deSmith has written that 'Parliament may by opt words expressly dispense with the need for notice or hearing although it is prima-facie requisite. It may permit enforcement powers against persons and property to be exercised expert. In the interests of administrative efficiency and expedition it has excluded the operation of the rule, wholly or in part, in various other contexts. It has enable decision-makers to hold undisclosed expert consultations or to refuse a hearing to an interested party or to decline to entertain particular kinds of objections or representations.

In G.C.H.Q. Lord Diplock declared that 'the executive government decided that the interest of the national security required that no notice should be given... the judicial process is totally inept to deal with the sort of problems which it involves'[141]

deSmith has enumerated the following factors on which a prima facie right to prior notice and opportunity be held to be excluded by implication. They are :

1) where the functions of the competent authority are held to be non-judicial.
2) where the authority is vested with a wide discretion.
3) where legislation expressly requires notice and hearing for certain purposes but imposes no procedural requirements for other purposes.
4) where the action taken constitutes denial of privilege as distinct from interference with a right.
5) Public interest
6) Prompt action, especially action of a preventive or remedial nature.
7) Impractibility of giving prior notice or opportunity to be heard.

---

140. Maneka Gandhi V. Union of India (1978) 1 S.C.C.291, per Bhagwati, J.
141. (1984) 3 W.L.R. 1174.

8) Availability of appropriate substitutes for prior notice and opportunity to be heard.
9) Trivial nature of interest.
10) Where the power exercised is disciplinary.

In the last mentioned factor, the author makes it clear that there is no general rule that courts will hold themselves aloof.[142] Maneka Gandhi and Mohinder Singh accepted the exclusion on the ground of urgency. The court has generally followed the general exclusions of the common law. However, we must remember that as Servar"[143] has pointed out, the British Parliament can exclude or modify the requirements of N.J. while in India any enactment excluding or modifying these requirements must stand the test of being consistent with fundamental rights. That is why our courts have urged that audi alteram partem rule must have a role in black listing, suspension, suppersession, absorption, Mal-practice in examination, Exclusion from institution and removal from post of service, because these all involve the fundamental rights of the citizens guaranteed in the supreme law of the land i.e. the constitution of India.

Effect of the Breach of the Audi Alleram Partem Rule

The effect of the breach of the audi-alteram portem rule is that the decision taken in violation of the rule is null and void, in the same way an any other Act which was utra vires. The duty to act fairly, just like the duty to act reasonably, was enforced as implied statutory requirements, so that failure to observe it meant that the administrative act or decision was out side the statutory power, unjustified by law and therefore ultra vires and void. The view is the logical conclusion drawn from Reidge V. Baldwin. Of course some of the law Lords in that case had opted for the word 'Nullity' instead of void. Lord Reid observed that "then there was considerable argument whether in the result the watch committee's decision was void or merely voidable. Time

---

142. deSmith, op. cit. 184-194.
143. Servant op. cit. 1444.

and time again in the cases. I have cited, it has been stated that a decision given without regard to the principles of natural justice is void and that was expressly decided in Wood V. Woad. I see no reason to doubt these authorities. The body with power to decide cannot lawfully proceed to make a decision until it has afforded to the person affected a proper opportunity to state his case"[144]. However, Lord Evershed argued that watch committee's decision was not void but voidable, and if the decision were merely voidable, the court need quash it only in case of 'a real substantial miscarriage of justice'[145]. Prof. Wade says that this would introduce dangerous uncertainty one might say, palm-tree injustice. Natural justice has for centuries been enforced as a matter of law and not of discretion[146].

deSmith says "Although breaches of natural justice used to be assignable as "errors in facts, a ground of challenge presupposing that the impugned order was merely voidable, there is a substantial body of recent judicial decisions to the effect that breach of the audi alteram partem rule goes to jurisdiction and renders an order or determination void. This is the better opinion"[147]. The learned author goes on to say that there remains nagging doubts whether breach of natural justice really does render an order or determination void. Three problems have been singled out in this regard. The first is retailing to waiver of the rules. The second is the thinking that a decision vitiated by the rules of natural justice can be made good by subsequent hearing. The third is if the breach of natural justice does not make any difference to the result what would happen? "The law is on this aspect still uncertain. In some cases the courts have refused to interface when satisfied that the outcome could not have been different had natural justice been fully observed. However, the learned author concludes that the decisions should not be allowed to stand in the absence of an adequate hearingl.[148]

---

144. (1964) A.C. 40 at p. 80.
145. Ibid. at p.91.
146. Wade, op. cit. p. 469.
147. deSmith. op. cit. p. 242.

In spite of the categorical assertion on the part of judiciary and academicians, the Privy Council held in ***Durayappah V. Femando***[149] that an order dissolving a council in contravention of the audi alteram partem rule was voidable but not anullity. If successfully impugned it would become void abinitio in relation to a person aggrieved and that the ex-mayor had no locus standi to impugn the order in his personal capacity, and that he would have had a legitimate interest in impugning the order had it been a nullity. The Privy Council relied upon the dissenting opinion of Lord Evershed and mis-quoted the judgement of Lord Morris of Borth-Y-Gest's. Prof. Wade has criticised the usage of the term 'voidable' in the following words : "Now however, the courts profess to have discovered a hybrid creature a voidable administrative act. This is a new animal in the legal bestiary and its pedigram is altogether questionable. By pursuing on a free rein judges have been able to propound new doctrine which would make far reaching changes in the law. This change, it will be submitted, would not only substitute new and worse rules for old and better rules on a number of matters, they would also gravely weaken the principle of legality which is the sheet anchor of the citizens right to resist unlawful acts of government[150]

In fact, the term voidable has been transplanted from the law of contract, where it had an intelligible part to play. into administrative law, where it has non, the term voidable, should never play a part in this field.

D.M. Gordon is of the view that the breach of the audialteram partem rule renders a decision voidable. There seems to be no logical justification for classifying a defect which a party can waive, as a defect of jurisdiction. Jurisdiction cannot be defective. It either exists or it does not. Non-observance of the procedure is error only"[151]

---

148. Ibid. 245.
149. (1967) 2 A.G. 337 P.C.
150. Unlawful Administrative Action, Void or Voidable Part I.83, L.Q.R. 1967,p. 499.
151. D.M. Gordon, 42 L.Q.R. at 523.

Akchurst M.B. is of the view that "a decision vitiated by breach of natural justice may be void for some purposes and voidable for others, but for more purposes the distinction between void and voidable decision in irreverent. This will clear away some old confusion, but it runs the risk of introducing new ones, for it forces words into unnatural meaning and underminds certainty multiplying the possibility of distinguishing earlier authorities[152].

The Privy Council observed in Calvin V. Carr that "A decision made contrary to natural justice is void, but that, until it is so declared by a competent body or court, it may have some effect or existence in law[153].

Dr. Markose regards the difference between void and voidable an unnecessary act. The void and voidable action is a clear case of abuse of power or discretion. Being cases of 'detournement de potivoin' the resulting decisions were void and statutory exclusion of judicial review could not have afforded any protection' [154]

The Privy Council held in **Attorney General V. Ryan**[155]" that a decision of the Minister which affected the right of the respondent was a nullity, as it had been arrived at in breach of principles of natural justice. Kelson[156]" has said that "it is a true annulment, an annulment with retro-active force. There must be something legally existing to which this decision refers it has to be considered as a norm annulled with retro-active force by the decision declaring it null abinitio".

Dr. Peter Brest has argued that the breach of the rule of audi-alleram partem makes the decision void. "Gross branch of the natural justice rules amounts to excess of jurisdiction"[157]

---

152. Waiver. 31 (1968) Modern Law Review 138 at 144-5.
153. (1979) 2 W.L.R. 755 at p. 763-65.
154. Dr.Markose, A.T.Public Law: Some aspects (1971) Edn.p.61.
155. (1908) 2 W.L.R.143.
156. 108 General Theory of Law and State, p. 131.
157. Cases on Constitutional and Administrative Law (1962), p.403.

Thus the breach of the rule is void and this declaration is a mean of controlling abuse of power by the executive government. Prof. Wade suggests that no logic can be extracted from void or voidable which will assist the resolution of cases. 'Void' is not an absolute but a relative term; a decision or act may be void against one person and valid against another.[158]

He further, says that there is no absolute kind of voidness. The reason is simply that no disputed act of a public authority can safely be treated as void in law unless the court can be persuaded condemn it.[159]

The Indian Thinking

The Indian thinking is not different from the British one. The order not complying with the principles of natural justice is said to be void, but in effect it has been treated only as voidable. It means that the order would have some effect and would exist in law until it is so declared by the competent body or court. This shows that the Indian Judiciary has accepted the doctrine of relatively of voidness propounded by Professor Wade. However, some judges have, held that such orders are not voidable but void only. Thus, Justice M.N. Beg observed in ***Sirsi Muncipality V. C.K. F. Tellis***[160]: "Violation of rules of natural justice results in a legally void decision". In Nawab Khan Abbas Khan V. State of Gujarat[161]" Krishna Iyer, J. observed: "An order is null and void, if the statute clothing the administrative tribunal with power, conditions it with the obligation to hear expressly or by implication. Beyond doubt an order, which infringes a fundamental freedom, passed in violation of audi alleram partem rule; is a nullity. When a competent court holds such official act or order invalid, or sets it aside, it operates from nativity, i.e. the impinged act or order was never valid. The French Jurists call it L, inexistence or out lowed order." He further suggests : "The law of jurisdiction and illegality has to be legislatively settled, not as

---

158. Prof. Wade, op.cit. p.471.
159. H.W.R. Wade, Unlawful Administrative Action, Void or Voidable. Pt. 84, 1968, L.Q.R. 95 at p. 109.
160. A.I.R. (1973) S.C., 855.
161. A.I.R. (1974), S.C., 1471.

logical extensions of judicial doctrine but empirical formulations based on experience. Grave implications of law and order bark behind this murky branch of public law.[162]

Beg, C.J. again observed in Maneka Gandhi V. Union of India: that the order of the Government of India impounding the passport of the petitioner was void became of the Lreach of the audi alteram partem rule. Majority in that case also observed that the impounding of the passport was clearly in the violation of the audi alteram partem rule, and that it was a fatal defect which could void the order. But the court, taking note of assurance by the attorney general on behalf of the Government of India that a time bound early opportunity would be given to the petitioner to make her representation, declined to interfere with the impoundment order. In **S.L. Kapoor V. Jagmohan and Swadeshi Cotton Mills' cases,** the Supreme Court held the order void on account of the breach of the rule, but declined to interfere on the basis of assurances of the post-decisional hearing.

Prof. M.P. Singh comments on the case in these words "The court has not recorded any sound or convincing reason for relegating the requirement of hearing to an expost-facto hearing in case of passports, as K.C. Davis has pointed out, unless the law expressly so provides the ex-post facto hearing can not be substituted for a prior hearing. Maneka Gandhi' thus modifies the Nawab Khan ruling to the extent that non observance of the principles of natural justice in reaching a decision affecting fundamental rights does not necessarily result in its nullity".[163]

Dr. S.N. Jain opines "'Void' and 'Voidable' are vague and imprecise words when a decision is void and when it is voidable is a highly mystifying part of the law. No articulated tests have been developed to furnish an answer. There is no unanimity on the question whether failure to observe audi alteram partem makes the decision void or voidable".[164]

---

162. Ibid, at 1477.
163. Administrative Action in Violations of Natural Justice affecting Fundamental Right (1979) 2 S.C.0 Journal Section, p. 1-8.
164. Is an Individual Bound by An Illegal Executive Order: Distinction between void and voidable Administrative Order J.I.L.I. 16, 1974,

However, in **Shridher V. Nagar Palika, Jaunpur**"[165] the Supreme Court very clearly held at p.310 that any order passed inviolation of principles of natural justice is rendered void. Similarly, the Supreme Court in **Bhagwan Shukla V. Union of India**"[166] held an action taken inviolation of audi alteram partem rule as invalid and quashed the same by issuing certiorari. The Rajasthan H.0 has also recently in **Banwari Lal V. State of Rajasthan** quashed an action taken in violation of hearing by issuing certiorari. The Supreme Court in State Bank of Patiala V. S.K. Sharma"[167] very recently gave a new dimension to the rule of audi alteram partem. In this case Supreme Court held that this principle of natural justice has many facets and a distinction ought to be made between violation of the principle of natural justice, audi alteram partem, as such and violation of a facets of the said principle. In other words there is distinction between "no notice", "no hearing" and "no adequate hearing" or to put it in different words, "no opportunity" and "no adequate opportunity". In the case of violation of a facet of the rule of natural justice, the validity of the order has to be tested on the touch stone of prejudice in such cases that is in violation of a facet of a natural justice the setting aside the order passed without further inquiry is not correct. The object of the principles of natural justice is to ensure that justice is done, that there is no failure of justice and that every person whose rights are going to be effected by the proposed action gets hearing.[168] Thus now the present position is that a decision in violation of facets of the rule of natural justice is not automatically invaid without further inquiry about the prejudice caused.[169]

Thus, the procedure adopted must be just, fair and reasonable in the particular circumstances of the case. In other words application of the principle of natural justice that no man

---

322.
165. A.I.R. (1990) S.C. 307.
166. A.I.R. (1994) S.C. 2480
167. A.I.R. (1996) Raj. 109.
168. A.I.R. (1996) S.C. 1669.
169. Ibid. at pp. 1881-82.

should from acting arbitraly effecting the rights of concerned person. It is a fundamental rule of any person without first being informed of the case and giving him and opportunity of putting forward his case. An ordered involving civil consequences must be made consistently with the rules of natural justice. The law must therefore be now taken to be will settled that procedure prescribed for depriving a person of livelihood or his other legal rights must meet the challenge of Article and such law would be tested on the and will of Article and the procedure prescribed affecting the civil rights would have to answer the requirement of Article. So it must be right, just and fair and arbitrary fanciful or oppressive. The manner of exercise or the power would also be in conformity with the principles of natural justice. Equality is the anti-thesis of arbitrariness, It is thereby, conclusively held by the Supreme Court that the principle of natural justice are the part of Article 14 and the procedure prescribed by law must be just, fair and reasonable.[170]

SECOND PRINCIPLE OF NATURAL JUSTICE - FREEDOM FROM BIAS

The second rule is that no man shall be a judge in his own cause. This is commonly known as the rule against bias. Lord Haldane stated in 'Arlidge' case that an administrative tribunal must "deal with the question referred to it without bias"[171]. It was emphasized that "The judges, like caeser's wife, should be above suspicion"[172] The principle underlying the rule against bias was clearly stated by 'Lord Cave' in Forme United Breweries V. Bath Justice. He observed in that case that "My Lords, if there is one principle which forms an integral part of the English Law, it is that every member of a body engaged in a judicial proceeding must be able to act judicially and it has been held over and over again that if a member of such a body is subject to a bias must be assumed, he ought not take part in the decision or even to sit

---

170. D.K.Yadav, V. J.M.A. Industries Ltd. JJ 1993 (3) SC617, (1993) 3 Sec. 259.
171. (1915) A.C. 120 at p. 132.
172. Leeson V. General Council of Medical Education etc.(1889) 43,Ch. D. 366; 385.

upon the tribunal. This rule has been asserted not only in the case of courts of justice and other judicial tribunals but in the case of authorities which. though in no sense to be called courts, have to act as judges on the rights of other"[173] At common law at earlier stages the rule that no man shall be a judge in his own cause was accepted as a just and reasonable solution of the problem. Sir *Nicholas Bacon:*[174] *the Earl of Derby,*[175] *the major of Hereford,*[176] *Brooks"*[177] *V. Earl of Rivers. Wright V. Crump,* [178] *city of London V Wood,*[179] *Dr Bonhams Case,*[180] *Day V. Savadge,*[181] are some of the cases: which clearly state the law of that time that common law did not permit a judge to determine a matter in which he had a direct pecuniary or proprietary interest. Braction"[182] asserted that a judge was not to hear a case if he was suspected of partiality because of consequinty, affinity, friendship or enimity with a party or because he was or had been a party's advocate. These principles were the canon Law Rules for the requisition of suspected judges which were applied in the English Ecclesiastical courts and also in medieval scottish courts. "They bear a close resemblance to the ground for disqualification of judges for likelihood of bias in modern English Law, Indirect support for an opinion that they were received into the common law might be derived from the fact that the grounds of exception for interest and bias to the competency of witnesses in courts christian had been applied from the earliest times. Yet there seems to be no evidence that Braction's broad statement of canon Law doctrine as common law was accepted and acted upon by his successors. Braction is not cited in any of the leading English cases on the matter. One must conclude that the balance of

---

173. (1926) A.G. 586, at p. 590.
174. (1563) 2 Dyer 220b.
175. (1697) 1 Salk.396.
176. (1668) Hardres 503.
177. (1702) 2Lord Raym 766.
178. (1701) 12 Mod. 669, 687.
179. (1610) 8 Co. Rep. 113b at 118a.
180. (1614) Hb. 85, 86. 87.
181. 133 (1614) Hab. 85, 86, 87.
182. DeLegibus. f. 412

probability is tilted against the view that the canon law rules were ever directly incorporated in the common law"[183] Thus, it is clear that at common law the judges did not directly incorporated the common law rules but they moved independently towards a just and reasonable solution. There was reluctance on the part of judges to recognise the concept of disqualification of judges for interest or bias. Sir Edward Coke asserted that judges and justices, unlike jurors, could not be challenged.[184] Blackstone also held that "for the law will not suppose the possibility of bias or favour a judge, who is already sworn to administer impartial justice, and whose authority greatly depends upon that presumption and idea"[185]. It is also not disputed that parliament is competent to make a man judge in his own cause. It was also asserted that "by taking the oath of office as a judge, a man ceases to be human and strips himself of all predilections, becomes a passionless thanking machine.[186] But this is doubtless a myth.[187]

The courts began to uphold the common law tradition by providing such a construction that such judges, as have interest in a particular case, are disqualified to be a judge. Whenever. circumstances point out that there is real likelihood of bias whether conscious or unconscious in relation to a party or an issue before him, the judge is supposed to be biased and he is not allowed to sit as a judge in such proceeding.

Kinds of Bias

There are mainly three kinds of bias :

(1) Official bias (2) Personal bias (3) Pecuniary bias.

1) **Official bias :** In the case of official bias, the officer is not actuated by any personal He is so imbued with the desire to promote the departmental policy that the becomes blind to

---

183. deSmith, op. cit. 249.
184. Co. lilt, 294a.
185. Comm. iii, 361
186. Re J.P.Linaham, 138 P. 2d 650 (1942) per Jerecome Frank J. R. V. Branslay Licensing JJ (1960) 2.Q.B. 167, per Devlin L.J..
187. DeSmith op. cit, p. 252

the existence of the interest of the private individual[188]. Official bias is the case of the previous connections of a judge with the material facts of the case by virtue of the office he one time undertook to perform in connection with those facts in some other capacity or context. The principle of official bias is not applicable when one of the members of a collective body has done something previously in his administrative capacity and later on some other members of that collective body take up the matter to decide in a judicial capacity. Thus in Mahesh Prasad V. Abdul Khair"[189] the Allahabad H.C. ruled that a person cannot be a judge in his own cause was not held to be applicable to a writ petition filed against the order of the Chief Justice or any other judge of the High Court acting in an administrative capacity. In Mary Fersea Dias V. Hon'ble Acting Chief Justice and Others[190], the Keral High Court opined the same and invoked the doctrine of necessity which authorise a judge to act where no other judge has jurisdiction even if he is disqualified otherwise. In a recent case, when Rajasthan Vidhan Sabha was adjourned sine die and a writ petition was filed in the Rajasthan High Court, the petioners prayed in the court that since one of the judges belonged to the ruling party at a particular time, he should not sit in the Bench because he was biased against the opposition party.

2) The High Court, however, did not agree with this view and held that the previous relationship of a judge does not disqualify him, when such a judge is not biased one.[191] The Supreme Court was also confronted with this problem in **Sheonandan Paswan V. Bihar,**[192] where it was held that the prosecutions against the Chief Minister of Bihar had been validly withdrawn. A review petition was field, and one of the grounds was that Mr. Justice Bahrul Islam, who was one of the judges of the Bench, had subsequently resigned his

---

188. A.T.Markose, Op. CIT, p. 217.
189. A.I.R. 1971, All. 205.
190. A.I.R. (1985), Kerala, 245.
191. The Times of India. 1986, p.
192. A.I.R. (1983). S.C. 194.

judgeship to contest election to the Assam Legislative Assembly on the ruling party's lieket and had been elected and was now a minister in the Assam Cabinet. Since his nomination papers were filed 46 days before he was due to retire, there was a likelihood of bias. The Supreme Court admitted the writ and a bench was constituted consisting of Justice Tutzapurkar, Justice R.B. Mishra and A.R. Sen, J.J. to hear the matter.[193] The Supreme Court did not categorically answer the question whether was real apprehension of likelihood of bias but upheld the decision of the previous bench. The court observed that it had approached the whole case in a purely 'detached manner'. The court was of the view that Mr. Sheonandan Paswan was political rival of Dr. Jagannath Mishra. There was no love last between them. It was at the instance of 'such a highly interested person' that this court was called upon to direct re-trial of the case, after setting aside the consent by the special judge.[194]

3) **Personal bias,** : Personal bias is purely a psychological process. It can arrive from diverse courses. Its positive side consists in a soft corner in the mind of the judge for one of the parties and may arise from personal alliances or from kingship or from sentimental affinities or from emotional inclination or from close associations between the judge and a party. The negative side consists in a hated malice, enmity or in the mind of the judge for either party. The most obvious in this line is the existence of blood or marriage relationship between any member of the tribunal and any one or more of the parties. The court has to be very careful to fix the quantum of suspicions sufficient to disentille a person from being the tribunal. For example, a tribunal whose members are against cow-slaughter should not be allowed to try a butcher or that a teetotaler should not be permitted to judge a drunkard."[195'] deSmith says that Personal Hostility,

---

193. Indian Express, April 14, (1983), p.
194. The Times of India Dec. 23, (1986) p.
195. A.T. Markose, op. cit. 215.

Personal Friendship, Family Relationship, Professional, Vocational Relationship, Employer and Employee, are also the facts of personal bias.[196]

4) Thus personal bias makes a person unfit to become a judge and the test of the likelihood of bias in such cases is that whether a reasonable person, in possession of relevant information would have thought that bias was likely. The proper approach for the judge not to look at his own mind and ask himself, however, honestly am biased but to look at the mind of the party before him.[197] In Mineral Development Ltd. V. State of Bihar[198]. Where the petitioner company was granted licence to mine mica for 90 years in 1947 but the same was canceled in 1955, the proprietor of the company alleged personal bias against the Revenue Minister who took the decision on the basis of his opposing the Minister in the general election of State Assembly and defeated him. The court held that there was likelihood of bias. Similarly in ***Arjun Chaubey V Union of India[199]***, the appellant was dismissed from service on charges of gross indicipline. He was served with a notice to explain his conduct in respect of 12 charges out of which 7 related to the Disciplinary Authority who himself considered the explanation and also passed the ultimate order of diminished. The court held and said " "Evidently, the respondent no.3 (disciplinary authority) assessed the weight of his own accusations against the appellant and passed a judgement which is one of the easiest to pass, namely, that he himself was truthful person and the appellant a liar. In doing this he violated a fundamental principle of natural justice. The order of dismissal passed against the appellant stands vitiated for the single reason that the issue as to who, between the appellant and respondent

---

196. deSmith, op. cit. 264-270.
197. Ranjeet Thakur V. Union of India, A.I.R. 1987, S.C. 2386 at p. 2390- 91
198. 150 A.I.R. (1960) S.C..
199. AIR. (1984) S.C. 1356.

No. 3 was speaking the truth was decided by respondent No. 3 himself.152[200]

5) **Pecuniary bias:** Any direct pecuniary interest, however. small in the subject matter may disqualify a judge. At common law no man is qualified to adjudicate in any judicial proceedings in the outcome of which he has a direct pecuniary interest. The rule applies no matter how exalted the tribunal. The said principles are equally applicable to authority, though they are not Courts of justice or judicial tribunals, who have to act judicially in deciding the rights of others. The pecuniary interest is fatal, however, slight the interest may be in the subject matters of decision.

In ***A.K. Krapeak V. Union of India"***[201] selections were made from the Jammu & Kashmir State Forest Service to Indian Forest Service and Chief Conservation of Forest of Jammu & Kashmir was an exofficio member of selection Board and also a candidate. He was selected. His selection was challenged on the basis of pecuniary bias. The court issued certiorari and quashed the selection. Similarly in ***D.K. Khanna V. Union of India"***[202] the High court quashed the selection by issuing certiorari where son-in-law was the member of the selection committee and father-in-law was the candidate. However, in ***Ashok Kumar Yadav V. State of Hariyana"***[203] where two of the selected candidates were related to one of the members of the commission and one of the selected candidates was related to another member of the commission, the Supreme Court relaxed this rule to some extent. The Court held in this case that there can be no doubt that if a selection committee is constituted for the purpose of selecting candidate on merits and one of the members of the selection committee is closely related to a candidate, it would not be enough for such member only to withdraw from participation in the interview of the candidate related to him-but he must

---

200. Ibid. at pp 1357-58
201. A.I.R. (1970) S.C. 150.
202. A.I.R. (1973) H.P. 30.
203. A.I.R.(1987) Sc. 454.

withdraw altogether from the entire selection process and ask the authority to nominate another person in his place. But situation in cases of public service commission is a little different. Commission consists of a chairman and a specified number of members and is a constitutional authority. In such situation the members of a public service commission are functioning not as individuals but as the public service commission. When a close relative of a member of a commission is appearing for interview, such member must withdraw from participation in the interview of that candidate and must not take part in any discussion in regard to the merits of that candidate and even the marks are credits given to that candidate should not be disclosed to him.

THIRD PRINCIPLES OF NATURAL JUSTICE. THE REASONED DECISION:

Reasoned decision has been described by the Donoughmore Committee, commonly known as committee on Minister's power as the third principle of the concept of natural justice. The Franks Committee noted that "almost all witnesses have advocated giving of reasoned decision by tribunal[204]. It considered that giving of reasoned decision was necessary if administrative procedure was to be fair to the citizen. Failure to state reason would totally frustrate such right of appeal an might exist. Reasons were more likely to have been properly thought out if they had to be stated in writing.

The general rule is that there is no duty to state reason for judicial and administrative decision. A statement of reasons is not required by the rules of natural justice.[205'] Therefore, there is no duty to state reason for the decision of the domestic tribunals. Even in the days before the Service Act of 1843. justices of the peace were never required to state reasons for their decision. Prof. de Smith says that "There is no general rule of English Law that reason must be given for administrative decisions"[206]. Prof.

---

204. Cmnd 218 (1957) paras 98 and 351.
205. Fontaine V. Chastarton (1968) 112 Solicitor General, 690: R. V. Gaming Board. See also (1970) 2 Q.B. 417; (1981) 1 WLR 754.
206. deSmith, op. cit. p. 486

Wade says the same and argues that it has never been a principle of natural justice that reason should be given for decisions. Since there is no such rule even in the courts of law themselves, it has not been thought suitable to create one for administrative body.[207] C.K. Alen also says that there is no general rule of the English Law to state reasons.[208]

The early cases also confirm this statement of law, Thus in Re Beloved Wilkischarity, Lord Truro, L.C. said that "I should say as a general rule, that the court ought not to require persons to state reasons for conduct which they are authorised to pursue."[209]

Sir R. Matins V.C. said the same in **Hayman V. Governors of Rugby School**[210]. In **Sharp V. Wakefield**[211] Lord Bram Well said that the magistrates are not bound to state their reasons. He argued that ministerial tribunal should not give reasons. Minister is the person whose opinion, is to govern and he must form it, itself on such reason and grounds as seen good to him, what use can the court make of the reasons if given. The Australian High Court has held the same in **Moreau V. Federal Commission of Taxation.**[212] In Chicago B.Q.R. Co. V. Babcock"[213] the Supreme Court of America also observed the same. In **Pure Spring Co. Ltd. V. Minister of National Revenue;**[214] Thorson P. of Exchequer Court of Canada has held the same. The **House Df Lord in Liversidge V. Andersonn**[215] held that Secretary of state did not have disclose the grounds of his belief and the court had no right to inquire into it. In **Green V. Secretary of State for Home Affairs**[216] , Lord MacMillian held that the Secretary of state is not bound to disclose, or to justify to any court the grounds on which he

---

207. Wade, op. cit, p. 486
208. C.K Allen Law and Orders. 3rd Fd. 1965, p.242.
209. (1851) 3 M.A.C. & G. 440-42 E.R. 330.
210. (1874) L.R. 18 F.Q. 28 p. 68-69.
211. (1891) A. C. 173 at p, 183.
212. 116g114.C. 173 at p. 183
213. 39 C.L.R. 65
214. 1, D.L.R. 501 at p. 534-39
215. (1941) 3. All. E.R. 338.
216. (1941) 3, All. in E.R. 388 at p. 396.

conceived himself to have reasonable cause to believe. The same was held in In *Point of Ayrecollieries Ltd. V. Lloyd George*[217].

However the court has made a difference between grounds and reasons. While there is no duty on the part of magistrates and authorities to state reasons for their decisions, they have not unlimited discretion to imprison. It has been held in R.V. Sykes "The justices may not be obliged to state reasons, they ought to state the grounds[218]. The same has been held in R. *Lancashire J.J. Exp. Tranter*[219], and in *R. V. Thomas*[220].

Indian Position :

Dr. S.N. Jain, opines that giving of reasons by the administrators for its action against the individual minimises chance of arbitrariness on its part and abuse of power by it.[221]

Our Supreme Court followed the English tradition in concluding that duty to give reason is not an integral part of natural justice. Apart from any requirement imposed by the statutes or statutory rule. either expressly or necessary implication. it cannot be said that there is any general principle or any rule of natural justice that a statutory tribunal should always and in every case give reasons in support of its decision. However. this vacillation on the part of the Supreme Court ended and court began to stress that it was obligatory on quasi-judicial authorities to give reason for their decisions In *Traven Core Rayans. V. Union of India"*[222] the court observed that necessity to give sufficient reason which disclosed proper application of the problem to be solved and the mental process by which the conclusion is reached in cases where a non-judicial authority exercises judicial function is obvious.

Prior to this case, the court held in *Mahabir Prasad V. State of U.P.*[223]*:* "Recording of reasons in support of a decision on

---

217. (1943) 2, All. E.R. 546
218. (1875) 1 Q.B.D. 52
219. (1887) 3 T.L.R. 678
220. (1890) 1 Q.B. 426.
221. 16, J.I.L.I. (1974) 142.
222. A.I.R. (1971). S.C. 862
223. A.I.R. (1970), S.C. 1302

a disputed claim by a quasi-judicial authority ensures that the decision is reached according to law and is not the result of caprice, whims ..? or fancy or reached on the grounds of policy or expediency.[224]

The other cases of this period are **Hari Nagar Sugar Mills V. Shyam Sunder**[225]; **Sardar Govindrao V. State of M.P.**[226] **Bhagat Raja V. Union of India**[227]. However, the court in **M.P. Industries V. Union of India"**[228] and **Som Datt V. Union of India"**[229] did not regard the giving of reasons essential. In **Bhagat Ram V. State of Punjab"**[230] the court agreed with the general proposition of law that it is not only desirable but also essential that the State Government should indicate its reason for forming its opinion under the *Act.* In **Mahabir Jute Mills V. Shibbon La1;**[231] Siemon Engineering & **Manufacturing Col. V. Union of India;**[232] **Rangnath V. Daulat Rao.**[233]" it has been held that every quasi-judicial order must be supported by reasons.

In **Union of India V. Tulsi Ram Patel**[234] the court observed that the disciplinary authority should record in writing its reason for its satisfaction. This is a constitutional obligation and if such reason is not recorded in writing, the order dispensing with the inquiry and the order of penalty following there upon would both be void and unconstitutional. The court further observed that it would, however, be better for the disciplinary authority to communicate to the government servant its reason for dispensing with the inquiry.

It would enable the government servant to approach the High Court under Article 226 or in a fit case, this court under

---

224. Ibid at 1304
225. A.I.R. (1961) S.C. 1169
226. A.I.R. (1965) S.C. 1232.
227. A.I.R. (1967) S.C. 1606
228. A.I.R. (1966) S.C. 671
229. A.I.R. (1959) S.C. 414
230. A.I.R. (1972) S.C. 1571.
231. A.I.R. (1975) S.C. 2057.
232. A.I.R. (1976) S.C. 1785.
233. A.I.R. (1975) S.C. 2146.
234. A.I.R. (1985) S.C. 1416.

Article 32. In *Anil Kumar V. Presiding officer and others"*[235] the Supreme Court observed that where a disciplinary inquiry affect the livelihood and is likely to cast a stigma, it has to be held in accordance with the principle of natural justice, the minimum expectation is that the report must be a reasoned one. The court then may not enter into the adequacy or sufficiency of evidence. It has to be a speaking order in the sense that the conclusion is supported by reason,'

The court held in *R.D. Shaft V. Union of India"*[236] that it is not the requirement of Article 311(2) of the constitution of India or of the Rules of natural justice that in every case the appellate authority should in its order state its own reasons except where the appellate authority disagrees with the finding of the disciplinary authority. Thus the court here makes it clear that requirement of giving reason is necessary only where the appellate authority disagrees with the findings of the tribunals. The court observed in *Ramchander V. Union of India"*[237] "We wish to emphasize that reasoned decisions by tribunals,... will promote public confidence in the administrative process, Considerations of fair play and justice also require that such a personal hearing should be given.[238]

The Supreme Court has held that recording of reasons is imperative for the fair and equitable administration of justice. The court observed in *V. V. Saraf V. New Education Institute"*[239] "This recording of reasons in deciding cases or applications affecting right of parties is also a mandatory requirement to be fulfilled in consonance with the principles of natural justice. What is imerative is that the order must in a nutshell record the relevant reasons which were taken into consideration by the court in coming to its final conclusions and in disposing of the petition or the cause by making the order".

---

235. (1985) LAB IC 1219, Supreme Court.
236. AIR. (1986) S.C. 1040.
237. A.I.R. (1986) S.C., 1173
238. Ibid. at p. 1182.
239. A.I.R. (1986) S.0 2105 at p. 2109

The Supreme Court has very clearly held in *S.N. Mukherjee V. Union of India"*[240] that keeping in view the expending horizon of the principles of natural justice, the requirement to record reason can be regarded as one of the principles of natural justice which govern exercise of power of administrative authorities and an administrative authority exercising judicial or quasi-judicial function is required to record reason for its decision, However, the court made it clear that the appellate or revisional authority, if it affirms the original reasoned decision, need not give separate reasons if it agrees with the reasons contained in the order under challenged[241].

LEGITIMATE EXPECTATION

A possibly fourth principle of natural justice is legitimate expectation. The State and all its instrumentalities have to conform to Article 14 of the Constitution of which non-arbitrariness is a significant facet. There is no unfettered discretion in public law. A public authority possesses powers only to use them for public good. This imposes the duty to adopt a procedure which is fair play in action. Due observance of this obligation as a part of good administration raises reasonable or legitimate expectation in every citizen to be treated fairly in his interaction with the State. To satisfy this requirement of non-arbitrariness in a State action, it is necessary to consider and give due weight to the reasonable or legitimate expectations of the persons likely to be affected by the decision or else that unfairness in the exercise of the power may amount to an abuse or excess of power apart from affecting the bonafide of the decision in a given case.

The concept of legitimate expectation stepped into the English Law in *Schmidi V. Secretary of State for Home Affairs"*[242] where in it has observed that an alien who had been given leave

---

240. A.I.R. (1990) S.C., 2105 at p. 2109
241. See also Bhagat Raja V. Union of India, A.I.R. (1967) S.C., 1606, Travan Core Rayons V. Union of India, A.I.R. (1971) S.C., 862, Narayan Das V. State of M.P., A.I.R. (1972) S.C., 2086, Union of India V. M.L. Kapoor, A.I.R. (1974) S.C. 87, and Mahabir Prasad Dwivedi V. State of U.P. A.I.R. (1992), All. 351.
242. (1969) 2 Ch. 149 Union V. Minister for the Civil Service (1984) 3 All, E.R. 935.

to enter the United Kingdom for a limited period had legitimate expectation of being allowed to stay for the permitted time and if that permission was revoked before the time expires, that alien ought to be given an opportunity of making representation. Thereafter, the concept has been considered in a number of cases.[243]

Thus the claim based on the principle of legitimate expectation can be sustained and the decision resulting in denial of such expectation can be questioned provided the same is found to be unfair, unreasonable and arbitrary.[244] In Food Corporation of India's case Justice J.S. Verma observed : "In a case of legitimate expectation if authority proposes to defeat a persons legitimate expectation, it should afford him an opportunity to make representations in the matter.[245] Hence, the doctrine of legitimate expectation has an important place in the developing law of judicial review[246]. On examination of some of these important decisions it is generally agreed that legitimate expectation gives the applicant sufficient locus standi for judicialreview"[247] and in a given case denial of legitimate expectation amounts to denial of right guaranteed and thesame can be questioned on the well known grounds attracting Article 14 of Constitution. The concept of legitimate expectation is therefore latest recruit to a long list of concepts fashioned by the Court for the review of the administrative action.

(D) ABUSE OF DISCRETIONARY POWER

It is far from clear to what extent certiorari is an appropriate means of challenging the exercise of discretionary powers by an administrative tribunal. It is a well-known

---

243. A.G. of Hong Kong V. Ngyuen Shiu (1983) 2 A.C. 629 and Council of Civil Services.
244. Navjoyti Co-operative Group Housing Society V. Union of India, A.I.R. (1992) S.C.W. 3075: and Food Corporation of India V. Kamdhenu Cattle Beed Industries A.I.R. (1993) S.C.VV, 1509.
245. Ibid Paras 7 and 8.
246. Findlay V. Secretary of State for the Home Department(1984) 3 All. E.R., 801.
247. Union of India V. Hindustan Development Corporation A.I.R. (1994) S.C. 988 at 1079.

principles of law that in the exercise of a discretion relevant considerations must be taken into account and irrelevant consideration disregarded. But if a tribunal infringes this principle, it is doubtful whether certiorari will issue to quash its decision. This doubt arises on account of a recent case, **R. V. Paddington & St. Marylebone Rent Tribunal**[248], ex-parte Kendall Hotels Ltd, where the landlords asked for certiorari to quash a decision of a rent tribunal on the ground that the tribunal had fixed the rent without having taken relevant considerations into account and at an arbitrarily low figure. The tribunal had statutory authority to fix the rent in its discretion. The court dismissed the applications holding that what was done is within the jurisdiction and therefore could not be challenged by certiorari.

The concept of abuse of powers deserves careful analysis. An administrative authority possessing discretionary powers must act according to law. The authority does not do so if it exercises its power for a purpose different from the one for which the power was conferred, or for an improper purpose, or acts in bad faith. or takes into account irrelevant considerations or leaves out relevant consideration, or the discretion is not exercised for the purpose contemplated by the statute or acts unreasonably. Failure by authority to follow, the mandatory procedure of the statute will also vitiate the exercise of discretionary power"[249] It is a well-known principle of law that in the exercise of a discretion relevant consideration must be taken into account and irrelevant consideration disregarded. The courts, tribunals and administrative bodies have a duty to exercise there statutory discretions one way or the other when the circumstances calling for the exercise of those discretions arise. Wrongful refusal to exercise discretion in such circumstances is a breach of duty redressible by an order of certiorari. It is a very well established principle of law that even

---

248. (1947) All E.R. 448.
249. Indian Law Institute Publication : Cases and Materialson Administrative Lawin India, Vol. I, (1966) at 637.

the widest discretion conferred by law is subject to judicial control on grounds of abuse of power, that is, malafides, improper purpose, extraneous conside-rations, leaving out relevant considerations etc. irrespective of the fact weather the function is quasi-judicial or administrative.[250]

The role of the courts in interfering with the discretionary powers of the Government is limited. Their duty is to ensure that the discretion has been exercised according to law. The Supreme Court has stated the position as follows :

"the court is not an appellate forum where the correctness of an order of Government could be canvassed. and, indeed, it has no jurisdiction to substitute its own for entirety of power, jurisdiction and discretion is vested by law in the Government. The only question which could be considered by the court is whether the authority vested with the power has paid attention to or taken into account circumstances, events or matters wholly extraneous to the purpose for which the power was vested, or whether proceedings have been initiated malafide for satisfying a private or personal grudge of the authority."[251]

The direction of the court will be to hear and determine according to law, though in some cases the application has been rejected on account of irrelevant considerations, the court may direct the authority, to grant the application.[252] " This may happen when the range of discretion has been cut down to such an extent that only one decision is possible.

Thus, concept of abuse of discretionary powers deserves careful analysis. Today it is often used in an omnibus term to over many things. From the point of view justice categories abuse of jurisdiction is distinct from excess of jurisdiction. A foolish

---

250. S.N. Jain - New Trends in Judicial Control of Administrative Discretion - (1969). 4 J.I.L.I. 540 at p. 552.
251. Pratap Singh V. State of Punjab, A.I.R. (1964) S.C. 72 at p. 83, See also Veerappa Pillai V. Raman and Raman, A.I.R. 91952) S.C. 192, Basappa V. Nagappa, A.I.R. (1954) S.C. 440, Mahboob-Sherif & Sons V. Mysore State Transport Authority, A.I.R.(1950) S.C. 321; State of Bombay V.K.P. Krishanan. A.I.R. (1960) S.C. 1223.
252. See Ahmedabad Manufacturing & Calico Ptg. Ltd. V. Municipal Corporation of City of Ahmedabad, A.I.R. (1956) Bomb.117.

tribunal may travel beyond its permitted boundaries. This may be due to ignorance. But abuse of jurisdiction seldom results from ignorance. If an abuse of jurisdiction is carefully analysed it will be found that either the tribunal intentionally misused the power for a different purpose from that for which it was conferred or the tribunal was recklessly careless of what it did and its effect on the individual. In the first case it may be said that the power is used for a collateral purpose and in the second case that the action of the tribunal was arbitrary or unreasonable[253].

There are many cases in Indian Administrative Law where through certiorari abuse of discretion have been prevented. Thus orders of tribunals which did not wait even for fifteen minutes to hear a party"[254] which resorted to its own theories to assess the premises of people,[255] which succumbed to political influences"[256] have all been quashed. **Krishnappa V. Bangalore City co-operative Bank. Ltd.**[257] deserves a brief notice. In this case the High Court quashed the decision of a co-operative society taken in abuse of its powers to expel a public spirited member. It is interesting to note that the illegal action of the authorities was upheld by the Government. Had not the High Court interfered the petitioner would have been remediless against the injustice about to be inflicted on him. In **Lalta Prasad V. Inspector-General of Police**, the attempt of Police authorities to make a travesty of a departmental inquiry against a subordinate who had to defend against grave charges was prevented by certiorari.[258] In a Rajasthan case the abuse

---

253. A.T. Markose : "Judicial control of Administrative Action in India", 1956. 202.
254. Devisikhamani V. Board of Commissioners for the Hindu Religious Endowments, Madras (1947) 2 M.L.R., 175.
255. Nanda Lal Bose V. Calcutta Corporation, (1885) 11 Cal. 275
256. Kandan Textiles Ltd. V. Industrial Tribunal, Madras (1949) 2 M.L 279; Cf. Surjan Singh V. Fakir Singh Ishwar Singh A.I.R. (1954) Nag. 107; The Rent Controller mad an order which in effect and substance substituted strangers as landlords behind the back of the real landlords!
257. AIR, (1954) Mys. 59.
258. A.I.R. (1954) All 438. The Police Act required notices and opportunity for cross-examination to be given tothose against whom departmental inquiries were launched. In this case cross-

disclosed was so plagrant that the High Court was constrained to warn the Magistrates concerned that they should remember that the constitution had come and that it was high time that they left off their "old time methods.[259]

(E) ERROR OF LAW

At one time it was thought that the courts had no power to interfere with a tribunal no matter how wrong the tribunal might be rules it had actually gone out of its jurisdiction. That was the case for about 100 years until in 1951, a case come before the English courts which altered the situation completely.[260] It arrest in this way : Upon the nationalisation of the hospitals one Thomas Shaw last his employment as clerk to the Northumberland Hospital Board. He was entitled by the regulations to compensation on a prescribed scale according to his length or service. The compensating authority granted him a sum which, was too little. They had failed to credit him with many years of service. He appealed to the compensation Appeal Tribunal. The tribunal dismissed his appeal, although he was entitled to a large sum. The tribunal had gone wrong in law. They had interpreted the regulations wrongly. Mr. Shaw applied to the Court of King's Bench for a writ of certiorari to quash the decision of the tribunal, and they did quash it. It was held that the court by the ancient writ of certiorari has inherent jurisdiction to control all inferior tribunals to keep them within their jurisdiction and also to see that they observe the law. The results was that the decisions of the Northumberland Compensation Tribunal was set aside and Mr. shaw got the compensation to which he was entitled.

The one defect in this is that the point of law has to appear on the face of the proceedings, "On the face of the record"

---

examination was positively refused and a notice of one hour was given of the charges.
259. Dhanwar Singh V. Sub-Divisional Magistrate, Khetri, A.I.R. (1953) Raj. 202, 204; a gem of an example is Ramanujam V. Commissioner. Corporation of Madras, A.I.R. (1955) Mad. 366.
260. R. V. Northumberland Compensation Appeal Tribunal (1952) 1 K.B.338.

as it is said. If the tribunal simply announce their decision without disclosing the point of law, certiorari is not available. This defect is bound up with the history of certiorari. At first the proceedings on summary convictions before justices had to be set out at great length. Everything necessary to support the conviction had to appear on the face of the record. The conviction had to recite the information in its precise terms. It had to see out the evidence of each witness as nearly as possible in his actual words. It had to state adjudication with complete certainty. It had to show that the case was brought within the terms of the Act of Parliament creating the offence. If there was any defect in point of form, or any error in point of law, appearing on the face of the record, the conviction would be moved into the King's Bench by certiorari and quashed. The result was that many convictions were quashed for highly artificial reasons. The legislature, therefore, intervened in 1848 to make the record of a convictions much more simple. Instead of a detailed speaking order, there was provided an unspeaking common order which rarely disclosed any error. This did not alter the law relating to certiorari but did make it impossible for the court to correct errors of law made by Justices except errors that went to jurisdiction. "The effect was not to make that which had been error, error no longer, but to remove nearly all opportunity of its decision. The face of the record "spoke" no longer, it was the inscrutable face of aphinx" (Per Lord Summer in R.V. Nat Bell Licuors Ltd.). This meant that in future the High Court quash by certiorari a magisterial determination only if a fundamental defect of jurisdiction was patent on the face of the record. This was one of the chief reason why the idea grew up and long persisted that certiorari was applicable solely to excess of jurisdiction. As a matter of fact it had always been the rule that certiorari would lie for error of law on the face of the record, as well as for error of jurisdiction. This was the principle established, or rather re-established, by R. V. Northumberland Tribunal Case discussed above.

The result of Northumberland case is that certiorari will extend to quash decisions which, though made within jurisdiction reveal on the face of the documents constituting the 'record' some error of law on which the conclusions depend. This is a valuable part of the High Court's supervisory function but if reasons for the impinged decision are not given it would appear that they cannot be compelled by certiorari and on that account a full use of this remedy may be impossible if those responsible do not give reasons on which it was based. This is an unfortunate limitation. The "speaking order" doctrine constitutes an unwarranted and illogical state of the law of judicial control that the effectiveness of review may depend on the readiness of the tribunals to volunteer written reasons, for their decisions, "Under the speaking order doctrine, if administrative agencies, in Lord Sumer's words "state more than they are bound to state, it may, so to speak, be used against them, and out of their own mouths they may be condemned".[261]

There are historical attachments to 'speaking order doctrine. Here it may be submitted that those limitations in the scope of the prerogative writs that are more historical attachments than anything else, should be removed. The speaking order doctrine is one such example. Another Crample speaking order doctrine is one such example. Another example is with regard to judicial or quasi-judicial acts. Certiorari could well be extended to administrative acts and decisions which are not of a judicial nature, so that, there too, what is wrong in law or done without authority could be quashed in a summary manner. Or, again. the High Court might be empowered, in the exercise of its prerogative jurisdiction, to direct the Minister or department concerned to state the reasons for a decision whenever those do not appear on the exhibited document.

The law relating to certiorari has often been criticised in recent years on account of the limitations mentioned above. In the United States, the author of the leading textbook on administrative law has written, "An imaginary system maximising fruitless litigation would copy the major features of the extraordinary remedies." It is submitted that various defects

---

261. K.C. Davis, Administrative Law (1951) p. 718.

which have gathered around certiorari could be minimised if the procedure laid down in Article 79 of the New York Civil Practice Act is adopted so that the moving party could, by a simple summary procedure, obtain whatever appropriate relief or to make a declaration of rights. One must remember that an aptand practical procedure is more than half the battle if the rule of law is to function effectively. Though Sec. 12 of Tribunal and Inquiry Act provides for reasoned decisions (ante discussed) but common rule is still unaltered.

The Supreme Court of India had followed Northumberland case in **Veerappa V. Raman"**[262] and held that certiorari is available on ground of error of law on the face of record, and such errors should be apparent on the face of record. Again in **Basappa V. Nagappa"**[263] the Supreme Court has held that an error in the decision or in determinations itself may also be amenable to a writ of certiorari but it must be a manifest error apparent on the face of the proceedings, e.g. when it is based on clear ignorance or disregard of law. In other words, it is patent error which can be corrected by certiorari but not a mere wrong decision. In this case Northumberland's case was followed. In India Case Law suggest that the ground of error of law has been constructed narrowly because errors of law must be manifest,[264"] or blatant, or so serious in their consequences as to shock Court's sense of justice. Recent case law also confirms this.[265]

In a decision Supreme Court has observed[266"] that it is difficult and inexpedient to lay down any general test to determine what errors of law can be described as errors apparent on the face of the record. Thus superior courts can review administrative action if there is an error of law apparent on the face of the record. In England first case where writ of certiorari issued against a decision of an Administrative Tribunal on the ground of error of law apparent on the face of the record

---

262. A.I.R. (1952) S.C. 192, 195.
263. A.I.R. (1954) S.0 440, 444
264. P.T. Service V. S.I. Court, A.I.R. (1963) S.C., 114.
265. Syed Yakoob V. Radhakrishna, A.I.R. (1964) S.C., 477.
266. Prem Sagar V.S.V. Oil Co., A.I.R. (1965) S.C., 111.

was R. V. Northumberland Compensation Appeal Tribunal.[267]" The first Indian case where writ of certiorari was issued against the decision of an Administrative Tribunal on the ground of error of law apparent on the face of the record was Han *Vishnu Kamath V. Syed Ahmed Ishaque*[268] where vote were counted against the provision of rule 47 (C) of the rules made under the Representation of People Act, 1951). The error of law which is apparent on the face of the record can only be corrected by certiorari. No error could be said to be apparent on the face of the record if it is not it self evident and requires an examination or argument to establish it. In *Ambika Mills V. S.B. Bhatt"*[269] Justice Gagendragadkar said that there is no doubt that it is only errors of law which is apparent on the face of the record that can be corrected and errors of fact though may be apparent on the face of the record can not be corrected. About error of law the Supreme Court in *Syed Yakoob V. K.S. Radhakrishnan"*[270] said that an error which has to be established by a long drawn process of reasoning on a point where there may be two opinions can hardly be said to be an error apparent on the face of the record that is error must be patent on the face of the records and no arguments are required to establish it[271].

(F) FRAUD

If the decision of an agency has been obtained by fraud or collusion, the decision may be quashed by issuing certiorari. There is no Indian case where certiorari has been asked on a account of fraud. In British Adminis-trative Law there are cases where on the ground of fraud certiorari has been granted. In *R.V. Gillyard"*[272] it was held that superior courts have an inherent jurisdiction to set aside orders made by inferior tribunals if they

---

267. (1952) 1. K.B., 338.
268. A.I.R (1959) S.C. 233.
269. A.I.R. (1961) S.C., 970.
270. A.I.R. (1964) S.C., 477
271. See, Veerappa V. Raman, A.I.R. (1952) S.C., Basappa V. Nagappa, A.I.R. (1954) S.C. 440 Shri Krishnan V. Kurukshetra University, A.I.R(1976) S.C., 376 and J. Jose Dhanpaul V. Thomas, A.I.R. (1996) 3 S.C.C. 587.
272. (1948) 2 Q.B.

have been procured by fraud or collusion a jurisdiction that now exercised by the issue of certiorari to quash. In ***Colonial Bank of Australia V. William"***[273] it was held that where fraud is alleged, the court will decline to quash unless it is satisfied that the fraud was clear and manifest and was instrumental in procuring the order impugned. Recently in ***Sanjay Kumar Singh V. Vice-Chancellor Purvanchal University"***[274] the Allahabad High Court declined to interfere under Article 226 of the constitution where the petitioner got his admission in M.Sc. (Ag) Part I (Animal Husbandry and Dairying) by manipulations in collusion with the Head of the Department concerned. Similarly appointment procedured against a reserved post by producing a false caste certificate, held, is wide and nonest and quashed[275]. Thus a writ of certiorari can be issued to correct a decision obtained by fraud or collusion.

Thus, a writ of certiorari can be issued for correcting errors of jurisdiction committed by inferior courts or tribunals, these are the cases where orders are passed by inferior courts or tribunals without jurisdiction or is in excess of it, or as a result of failure to exercise jurisdiction. A writ can similarly be issued where in exercise of jurisdiction confirmed on it, the court or tribunal at illegally or improperly, as for example, it besides a question without giving an opportunity to be heard to the party affected by the order or where the procedure adopted in dealing with the dispute is opposed to principles of natural justice. There is, however, no doubt the jurisdiction to issue a writ of certiorari is supervisory jurisdiction and the court exercising it is not entitled to act as an appellate court. This limitation necessarily means that findings of fact reached by the inferior court or tribunal as a result of the appreciation of evidence can not be reopened or quashed in writ proceedings. An error of law which apparent on the face of the record can be corrected by a writ, but not an error off act however grave it may appear to be. In regard to a finding of fact recorded by the tribunal, a writ of certiorari can be issued if it is known that in recording the said finding. The tribunal had erroneously refused to admit admissible and

---

273. (1974) L.R. 5 P.C. 417.
274. A.I.R. (1991) All. 21.
275. R.Vishwanatha Pillai V. State of Kerala. (2004) 2 SCC 105.

material evidence or had erroneously admitted in admissible evidence which has influenced the impugned finding. Similarly if a finding of fact is based on no evidence, that would regarded as an error of law which can be corrected by a writ of certiorari. In dealing with this category of this cases however, it must be kept in mind that a finding of fact recorded by the tribunal can not be challenged in proceedings for a writ of certiorari. On the long that the relevant and material evidence addused before the tribunal was in sufficient or in adequent to sustain the impugned finding.[276]

5 Chapter

PROBLEMS OF LOCUS-STAND1 IN CERTIORARI

(A) PROBLEMS OF LOCUS-STANDI

Locus- standi is a subject on which logically uniform decision can not be expected. Certiorari does not issue as "of right" or "of course". The term "of right" indicates that it cannot be had until dye grounds are shown. The term "of course" signifies that it cannot be had for the mere asking, without any grounds being shown. For more than two centuries, certiorari to quash has never been of course, except possibly for the crown. It has all along been treated as "discretionary" in the sense that the courts may refuse it even where the applicant makes out a prima facie case. In *1793, R.V. Basu"*[277] it was held to be discretionary in the court to grant or refuse a certiorari to remove a conviction

---

276. M/s Lakshmi Precion Screws Ltd. V. Ram Bhagat, JT 2002 (6) SC 162 at 164
277. 5 T.R. 351.

before justice of the peace. In ***R. V. Cambridgeshire JJ (1835)***[278]: the court held that in the exercise of its discretion it would refuse to allow a certiorari to issue if it considered that the matter could be decided by appeal. Again, in ***R.V. Manchester & Leads Ry (1838)"***[279] the court held that the issue of certiorari was a matter of discretion even though there may be fatal defects on the face of the proceedings it is sough to bring up. It is needless to cite other authorities for the proposition that certiorari is a discretionary remedy; but how and when the discretion is exercised is the real problem, bound up with the question of locus standi. In ***R.V. Survey J.J.***[280], where Justices had made an order that the repair of certain 'all necessary' reads should case, and that they should be stopped up, the statute in question provided that notices of the stopping up should appear at each end of the roads to be stopped up, and since notices had only appeared at one end of each of the roads, the order was void, as made without jurisdiction, certiorari being the proper remedy to bring up the order to be quashed.

The question then arose who should apply for the writ, and Blackborn question with approval Cockburn C.J. saying :

"I entirely concur in the proposition that. although the court will listen to a person who is a stranger. and who interferes to point out that some other court has exceeded it jurisdiction, whereby some wrong or grievance has been sustained, yet that is not exdebito justitiae but a matter upon which the court may properly exercise its desertion, as distinguished from the case of a party aggrieved, who is entitled to relief exdebito justitiae if he suffers from the usurpation of jurisdiction by another court."

It was thus laid down that an aggrieved person was entitled to the writ exdebito justitiae, whereas a 'stranger' has no such undeniable claim and is at the discretion of the court.

In ***R.V. Stafferd J.J., Ex. P. Stafferd Corp."***[281] this distinction was accepted by the Court of Appeal but with the

---

278. 4 A & B 111
279. 8 A & B 415.
280. L.R. 5 Q.B. 466.

qualification that even when the order is claimed exdebito justitiae, on the basis of individual grievance or interest, there is still a discretion in the court to determine whether the issue of the writ in the particular circumstances of the case is appropriate-whether, for example, it is effectual and enforceable or even whether it is deserve by the applicant. If this is correct, it follows that discretion extends over the whole are, of certiorari. In **R.V. Hendon R.D.C. Exp. D. Chorley**[282], where there was a decision of the Rural District Council to permit 'development' under a certain statute : one of the ouncilors present when the resolution to grant permission to develop was passed was biased and had such interest in the matter as to disquality him from taking part or voting, on account of bias, and so the council's decision was quashed at the instance of Professor Chorley, who was ratepayer. From this case it is clear that the discretion has at times been widely used. **Dr. C.C.M. Yardley has suggested"**[283] : "Could it be that, in fact, there is no problem of locus standi and that the distinction between a ' person aggrieved' and a stranger to the suit applying for a certiorari is purely an artificial one erected by the courts to express the truth which they have not realised themselves, namely, that the whole question of whether or not a certiorari shall issue is entirely within their own very wide discretion, whoever may be the applicant."

It is submitted that the above statement suggesting that even a stranger should be able to apply, even though he has no grievance of any kind, is a very wide one implying as it does that the courts would be willing to enter into abstract points.

Problem of Locus Standi in India :

The general rule is that it is the person whose right has been infringed can apply for a writ under Article 226. In the ***State of Orissa V. Madan Gopaf"***[284] Supreme Court observed as below :

---

281. (1940) 2. K.B. 33.
282. (1933) 8 K.B.696.
283. (1955) 71 L.Q.R. 388.
284. I.L.R. (1951) Hyderabad, 461 (S.C.)

"The concluding words of Article 226 have to be read in the context of what proceeds the same, Therefore the existence of the right is the foundation of the exercise of jurisdiction of the court under this Article".

Thus the relief under Article 226 is based on the existence of a right. The same, a fortiori, is the position in regard to Article 32 also. Thus, for instance, where a law infringes the fundamental right of a company, a shareholder cannot, normally, apply under Article 32 for the enforcement of the Company's fundamental right as, in the eye of law, the two are distinct entities. In ***Chiranjitlal V. Union of India***[285], Mukherjea J. of the Supreme Court observed as follows :

"It would not be open to an individual shareholder to complain of an act which affects the Fundamental Rights of the Company except to the extend that it constitutes an infraction of his own rights as well. This follows logically from the rule of law that a corporation has a distinct legal personality of its own with rights and capacities, duties and obligations separate from those of its individual members. As the rights are different and inhere in different legal entities, it is not competent to one persons to seek to enforce the rights of another except where the law permits him to do so. A well known illustration of such exception is furnished by the procedure that is sanctioned in an application for a writ of habeas corpus. Not only the man who is imprisoned or detained in confinement but any person, provided he is not an absolute stranger, can institute proceedings to obtain a writ of habeas-corpus for the purpose of liberating another from an illegal imprisonment To make out a case under this Article, it is incumbent upon the petitioner to establish not merely that the law complained of is beyond the competence of the particular legislature as not being covered by any of the items in the legislative lists but if affects or invades his Fundamental Rights guaranteed by the Constitution, of which he could seek enforcement by an appropriate writ or orders. The rights that could be enforced under Article 32 must ordinarily be the rights

---

285. (1950) S.C.R 869.

of the petitioner himself who complains of infraction of such rights and approaches the Court for relief."

(B) STATUTORY CURTAILMENT OF REVIEW OF CERTIORARI

Sometimes statutes purport to out down the right of judicial review of administrative decisions but so far as certiorari is concerned it is settled that the remedy by certiorari 'is never to be taken away by any statute except by the most clear an explicit words.' This is the ratio of the case *R. V. Medical Appeal Tribunal, exp. Gilmore,*[286] where the court of Appeal held that the remedy for certiorari was available to quash a decision of a medical appeal tribunal for an error of law on the face of the record, not with standing that section 36 (5) of the National Insurance Act, 1946 provides that : "......any decision of a claim or question shall be final." The facts were : In 1936 the applicant, a colliery pick sharpner, sustained an injury to both eyes while at work, his right eye being rendered almost blind. In March, 1955, he suffered a further injury at work, by which the condition of his left eye was so severely aggravated that in the result he was almost totally blind. The point of law on which the medical appeal tribunal was found to be in error related to the application of a regulation which deals with injury to one of two paired organs, such as eyes, legs, and hands. The Tribunal had failed to realise that once they had accepted aggravation to the left eye, they ought to have accepted the disablement not only for the left eye but also for the right eye which had been injured years before.

The applicant, after exhausting all the statutory ways of correcting the decision of the medical appeal tribunal, applied for an order of certiorari to quash the decision of the tribunal. The question arose whether the tribunal's decision, expressed by statute to be final, could be quashed on an application for certiorari. This was a question which had not been discussed by the same court in *R. V. Northumberland Compensation Appeal Tribunal exp. Shaw"*[287] because it not arise in that case. The

---

286. (1957) 1 Q B , 574.
287. (1952) 1.K.B. 338.

court held that the words, "any decision of a claim or question... shall be final" mean only that there shall be no further appeal. The formula does not exclude recourse to certiorari. It makes the decision final on the facts but not final on the law whether the error in law be an excess of jurisdiction or a mistake on the face of the record. Denning L.J. traced the history as follows :

"Lord Coke started this train of authority when he said that the words of an Act of Parliament "shall not bind the King's Bench because the pleas there are coramipso Rege." Kelynge C.J. gave the train an impetus in 1870 when an order of the Commissioner of sewers was brought before him. It was pointed out that the statute enacted "that they should not be compelled to certify or return their proceedings." Kelynge C.J. disposed of the objection saying "yet it never was doubted, but that this court might question the legality of their order notwithstanding; and you cannot oust the jurisdiction of this court without particular words in Act of Parliament. There is no jurisdiction that is uncontrollable by this court : ***Rex V. Smith, Calliaon Severs p.343.***

After citing various decisions, Denning L.J. concluded: "The remedy is not excluded by the fact the determination of the board is by statute made 'final'. Parliament only gives the impress of finality to the decisions of the tribunal on the condition that they are reached in accordance with the law." Prior to the enactment of the Summary Jurisdiction Act 1848, the court never doubted that the word 'final' did not take away the right of the King's Bench to bring proceedings before itself by certiorari. The Summary Jurisdiction Act by simplifying procedure, disarmed the exercise of certiorari as part of the supervisory jurisdiction of the High Court.

Thereafter a record of summary conviction no longer included any statement of the evidence and thus all opportunity of detection an error to quash was removed.

The Report of the Committee on Administrative Tribunals and Inquiries at para 167 states. "It is now clear that the fact that the decision of the tribunal may be expressed in the statute as 'final' does not oust its jurisdiction;" and again at para 117, the recommendation is that no statute should contain words purporting to oust remedies by way of orders of certiorari. prohibition and mandamus.

In India, the Supreme Court has observed in ***Kerala Education Bil1***[288], that any law seeking to take away or restricting the jurisdiction of the High Court under Article 226 must be held to be void and that the High Court shall be entitled to exercise the power under Article 226 free from the fetters imposed directly or indirectly.

PUBLIC INTEREST LITIGATION

The Indian Supreme Court has been struggling hard to innovate a new jurisprudence of access to justice and to evolve a new doctrine of accountability of the state for constitutional or legal violations adversely affecting the interests of the disadvantaged sections of society. Locus standi is a subject on which logically uniform decisions cannot be respected. The general rule is that it is the person, whose right has been infringed can apply for writ under Article 226. Similar is the position under Article 32 as has been observed by the Supreme Court in ***Chirantjeet Lal V. Union of India (AIR 1951 SC 41)*** that the rights that could enforced under Article 32 must ordinarily be the rights of the petitioner himself who complains of infraction of such rights and approaches the court for relief. Thus with regard to locus standi the traditional rule is that a person who has suffered a specific legal injury by violation of his legal right can only lying an action for judicial redress. This question of locus standi arises with all the prerogative remedies including the writ of certiorari. But in recent years the courts have evolved certain exceptions to the rule of locus-standi. The underline principle of such exception is that if a person is unable to approach the court on account of some disability or it is not practicable for him to move the court for some other reasons such as his socially or economically disadvantaged position, some other person can invoke assistance of the court for the purpose of providing to

---

288. (1959) SCR 995

judicial redress to the person wronged or injured, so that the legal wrong or injury does not go unredress.[289] Thus the emergence of public interest litigation that is litigation at the instance of a public spirited person exposing the cause of others has related the traditional rule considerably and by 1979 it become abundantly clear that the court was indeed in search of a new kind of constitutional litigation. The movement for liberalisation of locus standi was infact started by Justice Krishna Iyyer in 1975 when he allowed the Bar Council of Maharashtra to initiate proceedings against an advocate for professional misconduct"[290]. Then in Municipal Council Ratlam V. Vardhi Chand"[291] he (Justice Iyyer) upheld the right of the residents of certain locality in Ratlam to initiate proceedings against the Municipal Council. This new doctrine of access to justice was more forcefully asserted by Justice *Iyyer in Fertiliser Corporation Kamgar Union V Union of India"*[292] where the court accepted the standing of the workers to challenge the legality or validity of sale of certain plants an equivalent of factory by the management. In *State of Hariyana V. Darshara Devr"*[293] he characterised right to access to Justice as fundamental of all fundamental rights and in *Jolly Narghese V. Bank of Cochin"*[294] he transplanted Article 11 of the International Convent on Civil and Political rights into fair procedure component of Article 21 of the Constitution of India.

In the last in *S.P. Gupta V. Union of India"*[295] Justice Bhagwati has fully legitimised the liberalised rule of locusstandi in public interest litigation where he observed that to insist on

---

289. Bhagalpur Blinding Case, (1981) S.C. 228; Asiad Workmen Minimum Wage Case A.I.R. (1982) S.C. 1473; Dholpur Kamala Flesh Trade Episode (1981) 4 S.C. C. 1; S.P. Gupta V. Union of India, A.I.R. (1982) S.C. 1950.
290. Bar Council of Maharashtra V. M.V. Dobhokar, A.I.R. (1975) S.C. 2092.
291. A.I.R. (1980) S.C. 1622.
292. A.I.R. (1991) S.C. 344.
293. A.I.R. (1979) S.C. 856.
294. A.I.R. (1980) S.C. 470.
295. A.I.R (1982) S.C. 149.

traditional rule of locusstandi would, ineffect, mean denial of justice to the poormasses. No state has a right to tell to the people that because a number of cases of the rich are pending in the courts, it cannot allow others to approach the courts until the arrears are disposed off. The Supreme Court in **Bandhua Mukti Morcha V. Union of India**[296] again upheld the legality of public interest litigation for the purpose of securing to workmen a life of basic human dignity in enshrined in Article 21 of the Constitution. In essence, the public interest litigation develops a new jurisprudence of the accountability of the State for Constitutional and legal violation adversely affecting the interest of the weaker elements in the community including the most important right of life and personal liberty guaranteed by Article 21 of the Constitution. Today a vast revolution is taken place in the judicial process and the problems of poor coming to the forefront. The courts have to innovate new methods and devise new strategies for the purpose of providing access to justice to large masses of people who are denied their basic human rights and to whom freedom and liberty have no meaning.

The only way in which this can be done is by entertaining writ petitions and even letters"[297] from public spirited individuals was seeking judicial redress for the benefit of persons who have suffered a legal wrong or a legal injury or whose constitutional or legal right has been violated but who by reason of their poverty or socially or economically disadvantaged position are unable to approach the court for relief.[298] Not only this even the dignity of court is protected through PIL.[299] Thus now the problem of locus standi has been liberlised in writ jurisdiction including the writ of certiorari.

---

296. A.I.R. (1984) S.C. 802.
297. Nilima Priyadarshani V. State of Bihar, A.I.R. (1987) SC.2021.
298. See for example, M.C. Mehtra V. State of T.N., AIR 1999 SC 41; K.Babu V. State of W.B., AIR 1997 SC 610; Gaurav Jain V. Union of India, AIR 1997 SC 3021,
299. Delhi Judicial Services Association V. State of Gujrat AIR 1991 SC 2176, is the most important case in this regard.

Chapter 6

CONCLUSIONS

Now it is the appropriate stage to touch upon the various aspects including glaring defects, short-comings and deficiencies with regards to the law of certiorari.

Certiorari is an order issued by a superior courts asking an authority or inferior courts to transmit the records of proceedings in some cause are action to the superior court for its consideration. This writ mainly goes to judicial or quasi-judicial body. But in many cases, a serious violation of people's right may be made by an administrative agency, which may not come within the definition of judicial act. Courts can quash order of the administrative authority either on error of law apparent on the face or an excess or abuse of jurisdiction. Certiorari is however not available if the decision of agency. is not based on an substantial evidence. Certiorari is discretionary or may be granted when the impugned act is on face of it erroneous or raises question of jurisdiction or infringement of the fundamental right of the petitioner."[1]

A writ of certiorari can be issued against even a mere administrative body if its executive order is not inconformity with the rule of Jaw and if it is outside its powers. Rules of natural justice have to be observed and the authority should have applied its mind. If the impugned order negatives this factors, certiorari can issue."[2] If there is some other specific and sufficient remedy then the question of certiorari normally does not arise. In addition, it is well established that the negligence on the part of

---

1. Hindustan Steel Ltd. V.A.K. Roy, A.I.R.1970, S.C. 1401.
2. Champalal Binani V.C.I.T., A.I.R.. 1971, S.C. 645.

persons on whose behalf an applications has been made will exclude the issue of the remedy.

This limitations have been adversely commented by the scholar of English speaking words. All this led Prof. Davis to say "either parliament or the law Lords should throw the entire set of prerogative writs into the Thamos river, heavily weighted with sinkers to prevent them from rising again."[3] Lord Denning also in his Hamlyin lectures said "just as the pick and shovel is no longer suitable for the winning of coal, so also the procedure of mandamus, certiorari and action on the case are not suitable for the winning of freedom in the new age".[4]

But inspite of these defects it is felt that certiorari is still a beneficial remedy. It requires certain reforms and such reforms are suggested as under:

It is submitted that the audi atteraum portem should apply to every case where the person or property of a private individual is adversely affected by the decision of an administrative agency and that regardless of whether the decision be characterised as "judicial", "quasi-judicial", "administrative" or one affecting only a privilege and regardless of the extent to which discretion may be involved. The test should be that of the effect upon the individual concerned. It seems that in England and India, the ordinary courts of law have reached the limit of their inclination to enforce a general standard of procedural fairness in the exercise of statutory powers. Fifty years ago it could have been said that the doctrine of audi alteram partem had great potentialities for growth. It does not seem that such hopes can be entertained today. In the U.S.A the law has been carried some way beyond the point where English Law stopped short in the Arlidge case; and in several countries of the commonwealth the general principle that statutory powers may be exercised only after fair hearings is now well established. See, for example, the Canadian case - ***L' Alliance des Professors Ethioliquers V. Labour Relations Board of***

---

3. 61, Kol. L. Rev, 201, 204.
4. Freedom under the Law at p. 126.

Quchec."[5] It is submitted that so far as India and England are concerned, it would be useful to enact a simple and general code of procedure, a kind of administrative bill of rights in the light of needs of twentieth and twenty first centuries. The first provision of this should be that no man's liberty, livelihood or property could be taken from him unless he had first been heard in his own defence, and that this should apply to all statutory powers in default of express provision to the contrary. Exceptions would have to be specified, for their powers -such as the power to arrest a suspected criminal which are in a different class from those to which natural justice applies. And legislative powers, which affect the public generally and not merely one or more individuals, would have to be excepted. The United States of America has not only the 'due process' clause of the constitution, which applies in such cases, but also the Federal Administrative Procedure Act of 1946. An example of the combined effect of the Fourteenth Amendment and the Administrative Procedure Act in enforcing the essentials of fair procedure is Wong Yang Sung V. McGrath (1950). In France it is also the case that the power, for example, to cancel a license cannot be legally exercised without giving a proper hearing to the person affected.

Some Observations regarding India

In India we find lot of corruption and mal-administration within administration, particularly maladmini-stration is wide spread, and it can be said that the lack of appeal system within the administration is the cause for that. While officials have been armed with a lot of unlimited powers and discretion, corresponding rights of individual have not been evolved in proper manner. Here we do not have such inquiry like Frank Committee in England to look in to the deficiencies of administrative justice.

The present inadequacy of the administrative structure and the individual helplessness against authority in the matter of securing administrative justice have been widely recognised. The fact remains that the existing remedies against abuse of authority

---

5. (1954) 4 D.L.R. 161

by administration particularly in lower echelons are not available to the common man, for whom concept of equality before the law and social justice have at present little significance or value. All these things necessiate greater judicial control and this can be done by judicial creativeness by the courts.

The judgements of the courts exhibit lack of creativeness. As we have seen that Indian courts have practically followed the principles of English law governing the writ of certiorari inspite of wide language used in Art. 226. It is urged that political, social and economic conditions in India differ widely from England. Again integrity in administration, expertise knowledge of tribunals, strong public opinion, council on tribunals and Ombudsman etc. strengthen the administrative justice in England while in India we lack these things. It is urged that Judges must take into account all these things living law of a community requires that it should take into account social facts and legal norms of a community should be able to meet particular needs of the community. It is high time that sound principles in the spheres of administrative justice should be evolved in the light of Indian conditions. Our Administrative Law should be Indianised rather than following English Law. It is regretted that the courts in India have practically transplanted English Law governing the writ of certiorari without applying their mind, whether certain rules of English Law are suitable in India under the present context. It is submitted that a thorough investigation should be made regarding utility and relevance of English rules governing the writs in India. As it is interesting to note that English rules relating to certiorari have been criticized by English men themselves. It is urged that Supreme Court should take a pragmatic approach as Mr. Justice Holmes once said that 'Life of law is not logic but experience'. All this necessiate a code of Administrative procedure in India in the light of present state of affairs, that is, such rights are to be created in the individual as not to jeopardised social welfare programme and economic planning of the State.

Till such code is created, it is submitted, that there is a need for greater judicial control over administrative process. The dignity of man and significance of his freedom are the essential postulates of democratic way of life which the Constitution heralded and this can never be achieved without justice, social, economic and political enshrined in our Constitution. IN solving the problems that confront the path to socio-economic justice, liberty and freedom judges have to play their role without fear or favour, uninfluenced by any consideration of dogmas or isms.

Judges are the upholders of the dignity, defenders of liberties and protectors of rights under the common law as well as the rights guaranteed by the Constitution. There must be judges in the land, says Lord Denning "who are no respectors of persons and stand between the subject and any encroachment on his liberty by the executive". Judges by their decisions, have contributed greatly to the moving and developing laws; and present day society pledged to democratic way of life looks eagerly and sincerely for their decisions on laws to have the liberties of the people safe-guarded against all invasions either by the State or by any authority and individual.

Legislative, Executive and Judiciary are the three limbs of the government, of these three, judiciary is the most important because it has a supreme task of striking a balance among executive, legislative and the people. Thus, the judges have prominent part of playing in order to keep the democratic way of life a progressing, The law as instrument of social change does not become fully effective unless certain conditions are satisfied. The primary condition is the creation and maintenance of a good law enforcement machinery which would command the confidence of the people and be fair, quick and operable at cost which the average citizen can afford.

The preamble of our constitution secures to all citizens social, economic and political justice and also equality of status and opportunity. The rule of law also requires that poor and illiterate persons should be assisted enforcing their rights. Article 39-A also provides that State shall ensure justice on the basis of equal opportunity to all citizens. Because of these reasons the locus standi concept has been relaxed and any public spirited person has been allowed to file public interest litigation in good faith for preventing the violation of the rights of the poor. It is, therefore, submitted that in order to prevent violation of rights of disadvantaged persons the public interest latigation ruled be encouraged. In some foreign countries also the concept of PIL is being encouraged. Here, it will not be out of place to mention that recently Mr. Aharon Barak, Chief Justice of the Israeli Supreme Court said at New Delhi before a gathering which included many judges of the Apex court of India that what would the Supreme Court of India do if a PIL was filed seepaing direction to the Prime Minister to sack a minister who has been indicated of corruption? He further said that in all probability, it will dismiss the PIL questioning the locus standi whereas the Israeli Supreme Court, in a similar matter, has directed the Prime Minister of the country to sack an indicated minister. He further said that in matters of public importance every Israeli has been standi warrant[6] whereas in India even in case issue of writ of quo-warranto, Allahabad High Court has recently held that although the principle of locus standi is to an extent relaxed in a writ of quo-warranto but it is not abondoned altogether. These must be some connection between the petitioner and the appointment be challenges.[7] It is thus submitted that PIL should be encouraged and in matters of public importance every Indian should have locus Standi.

However, inspite of the limitations and short comings stated above the prerogative remedies in India have been largely availed of by the people to their great advantage. Article 226 of the Constitution has made the people feel that the State exists primarily for their good and that under its laws they have rights of which they can obtain quick enforcement by the highest court in the state at a very reasonable cost.[8] Not only this in case of violation of fundamental rights they can obtain quick justice by the Apex Court of the Country at a very reasonable time and cast

---

6. Times of India, 24.2.2004 p. 8.
7. Mahesh Chanra Gupta V. Dr. Rajeshwar Dayal, 2004 All. L.J. 257.
8. Law Commission of 1955 - Report (1918). Vol. II, p. 658.

and the courts do justice to the individual citizen while giving due weight to the requirements of the public interest and they feerlessly enforce the principle, that government must be carried on strictly in accordance with the law. It is, however, submitted that the scope of certiorari should be widened by adopting. The principle that administrative fact findings unsupported by substantial evidence should be liable to be quashed and any error of law involved in an administration decision should be capable of correction by certiorari even through it is not apparent on the very face of the record.

SELECT BIBLIOGRAPHY

Article

1. E.Will-Heim, "Legal representation before administrative tribunal", A.L.J.(1969) p. 64.
2. Gordon D.M. 42 L.Q.R. at p. 523.
3. Harry W.M. "The role of Lawyers in Administrative justice", 33 M.L.R. p. 481.
4. Indian Law Institute Publication - cases and material on Administrative Law in India, Vol. I (1986) at p. 637.
5. Jain S. N. "In an Individual bound by a Illegal Executive Order : Distinction between void and voidable administrative order" J.I.L.I. 16 (1974) p. 322.
6. Jain S. N. "New Trends in Judicial Control of Administrative Discretion".
7. Jain M. P. "Bias and Administrative Law, 13," J.I.L.I. (1969) 4 J.I.L. 154 (1971), p. 362.
8. Massey I.P. "Discretion to disobey invalid order", 1 S.C.0 (1978), p. 32.
9. Pound R. "The Administrative Application of Legal Standards" (1919) 44, A.B.A. Report, p. 445, 446.
10. Shukla S.N. "Grounds for Certiorari" (1960) S.C.J. 247 at p. 250.
11. Singh M.P. "Administrative action in violation of Natural Justice affecting Fundamental Right (1979)" 2 SEC Journal Section, p.1-8.
12. Wade, "Unlawful Administrative Action, void or voidable" Part I 83, L.Q.R. (1973), p. 499.
13. Wade, "Natural Justice and Disciplinary Inquiries" 84, L.C.R. 451.
14. Wade, "Unlawful Administrative Action, void or voidable", Pt. II, 84 (1968) L.Q.R. 95 at 109.
15. Waiver, 31 (1968) Modern Law Review 138 at 144, 145.

BOOKS

16. Allen C. K. "Law and Orders [Comparative Administrative Law," 6 Ed. Vol. 3.
17. Allen C. K. "Law in the Making"
18. Basu D. D. "Commentary on the Constitution of India", 6th Ed., Vol. 3

"Comparative Administrative Law"

19. Blackstone "Commentary" Vol. 3
20. Cawell H. "The History and Constitution of the Courts and Legislative Authorities in India"
21. Chaudhari A.S. "High Prerogative Writs" Vol. I
22. Craig P.P. "Administrative Law" (Second Ed.)
23. Denning A.T. "Freedom under the Law"
24. Denning A.T. "The Changing Law"
25. DeSmith S.A. "Judicial Review of Administrative Actions"
26. Devis K.C. "A Hand Book of Administrative Law"
27. Dubey H.P. "A Short History of the Judicial Systems of India and some Foreign Countries"
28. Faweel "The First Century of British Justice in India"
29. Fazal M.A. "Judicial control of Administrative Action in India and Pakistan"
30. Friedman "Principles of Australian Administrative Law"
31. Garner J.F. "Administrative Law"
32. Griffth and Street "Principle of Administrative Law"
33. Halsbury's "Halsbury's Laws of England", Hailsham Edition Vol. IX.
34. Henderson E.G "Foundation of English Administrative Law"
35. Holdsworth Sir W.S. "A History of English Law", Vol. I
36. Indian Law Institute "Cases and Materials on Administrative Law in Publication", India, Vol. I.
37. Jain & Jain M.P. & S.N. "Principles of Administrative Law" (Fourth Edition)

38. Jain M.P. "The Evolving Indian Administrative Law" (1983)
39. Jenks "The Prerogative Writs" (1923) 32 Yale L.
40. Jones B.L. "Garner's Administrative Law" (Seventh Ed.)
41. Joshi K.C. "Administrative Law"
42. Kagzi M.C. Jain "The Indian Administrative Law"
43. Katju Markandey "Domestic Enquiry"
44. Keslon "General Theory of Law and State", p. 131.
45. Louis L.Jaffe "Judicial Control of Administrative Action"
46. Maitland "History of English Courts"
47. Markose A.T. "Public Law : Some aspects" (1971) Edn. p.61.
48. Markose A.T. "Judicial Control of Administrative Action in India"
49. Marshall "Natural Justice"
50. Massey I.P. "Administrative Law"
51. Palkhivala N.A. "A Judiciary Made to Measure"
52. Peter Brest "Cases on Constitutional and Administrative Law" (1962) p. 403.
53. Rabson "Justice and Administrative Law"
54. Ramchandran U.G. "Administrative Law"
55. Sathe S.P. "Administrative Law"
56. Sathe S.P. "Administrative Law" (Fourth Edition)
57. Schwartz B "An Introduction to American to American Administrative Law"
58. Seatalwad M.C. "The Common Law in India"
59. Sheervai H.M. "Constitution of India"
60. Short and Millor "Crown Practice"
61. Shukla S.N. "Judicial Control of Administrative"
62. Shukla V.N. "Commenteries on India's New Constitution"
63. Thakker C.K. "Administrative Law"
64. Upadhyay J.J.R. "Administrative Law"
65. Wade and Phillips - Constitutional Law

66. Wade E.C.S. "Constitutional and and Broadley A.W. "Administrative Law".
67. Wade H.W.R. "Administrative Law towards Administrative Justice "

www.ingramcontent.com/pod-product-compliance
Lightning Source LLC
Chambersburg PA
CBHW020004050426
42450CB00005B/304